THE B O

North African
cooking

T H E   B O O K   O F

North African cooking

LESLEY MACKLEY

Photographed by
SIMON BUTCHER

HPBooks

ANOTHER BEST SELLING VOLUME FROM HP BOOKS

HPBooks
Published by The Berkley Publishing Group
200 Madison Avenue
New York, NY 10016

9 8 7 6 5 4 3 2 1

By arrangement with Salamander Books Ltd.

© Salamander Books Ltd., 1998

ISBN 0 84065 015 X

Home Economist: Nicola Fowler
Printed and bound in Spain by Bookprint, S.L.

CONTENTS

FOREWORD

The appearance of couscous and harissa on our supermarket shelves, and tagines and couscoussières in cookshops and hardware stores, is a sure sign that our passion for Mediterranean food has now extended to the shores of North Africa. An abundance of fine ingredients, the influence of the various civilizations who have passed through or settled in the area, and the innate hospitality and generosity of the North African people all combine to make this one of the most varied and interesting cuisines in the world. Fragrant stews of meltingly tender meat and dried fruits, hot and spicy marinated and grilled fish, saffron-scented couscous and rice, colorful salads and desserts of sun-ripened fruits and nuts cannot fail to tempt and delight.

With over 80 beautifully illustrated recipes, this book brings you the range and variety of North African cooking. Classic dishes such as Tunisian Brik with Tuna, Chicken Tagine, Moroccan Couscous, Bistilla and Marrakesh Serpent Cake are found alongside new ways with traditional ingredients such as Lamb with Mashed Chick-peas and Goat Cheese and Fig Dressing. There are dishes for every occasion and many are suitable for vegetarians, but whatever your taste, all the recipes will bring the color and flavor of North Africa to your table.

——— NORTH AFRICAN COOKING ———

The North African countries of Morocco, Algeria, Tunisia and Egypt have much in common in their styles of cooking. They share similarities of climate and landscape, but more importantly, a combination of different influences from the cultures of the ancient civilizations that invaded and traded along the southern shores of the Mediterranean Sea. North African cooking is a happy marriage of the cooking styles of the ancient Mediterranean, the Near East and Persia, whose influence is seen in the mixing of ingredients and spices. In addition, many ideas are borrowed and adapted from France and Italy and there is much evidence of Moorish history. Although in many kitchens the mortar and pestle has now given way to the food processor, most North African cooks are determined to pass their traditions on to future generations. Recipes have been handed down through the centuries and adapted to reflect regional and seasonal availability. As with all the Mediterranean countries, the North African diet is extremely healthy, with abundant fresh fruit, vegetables, salads, pulses, bread, herbs, olive oil, fish and broiled meat.

THE NORTH AFRICAN MEAL

Arabs are extremely hospitable and entertain warmly. Meals are expanded to accommodate unexpected guests and any visitor to the house is offered food and drink. Much of the cooking is done in company, with mothers, sisters and daughters all sharing in the food preparation. Although modern kitchens usually contain a gas or electric range, many cooks still prefer to cook outdoors on a charcoal brazier. Meals are leisurely and sociable and take place at low round tables. Food is eaten with two fingers and the thumb of the right hand and at a traditional meal each person dips into the same serving dish. A large variety of mezze is served before a meal, or to accompany drinks at any time. There may be anything from four to forty different dishes and can be as simple as nuts, cheese or pickles or miniature versions of main meal dishes.

Soups tend not to be served as a first course, but as a meal in themselves. They are often very substantial and are served with bread. Soup is sold in the streets early in the morning as breakfast for people on their way to work. A bowl of soup, especially harira, is the usual way to end the days of fasting during Ramadan.

A main dish could be a slowly simmered stew of meat or poultry with vegetables or broiled fish or meat. Salads and cold vegetables are present at most meals and couscous or rice and bread will also be served. For a special occasion a whole lamb might be spit-roasted over a fire, and the traditional couscous stew is usually served as a party dish.

Desserts, other than a bowl of fruit, are not normally eaten at everyday meals, but are saved for visitors and festive occasions, when sweet pastries, stuffed with nuts and bathed in syrup, are very popular.

Sweet mint tea is served at the end of a meal to aid digestion. It is served in brass pots and is poured through the long narrow spout into tea glasses. The serving and drinking of coffee is surrounded by tradition and is a very important activity. Men gather in cafés to drink strong coffee, often flavored with cardamom, in tiny cups, and any visitor is always greeted with freshly made coffee, brewed in long handled copper or brass pots called ibriks.

Sweet syrupy drinks and sherbets are very popular and are widely sold on the streets. Alcohol is prohibited by Muslim dietary laws, but as a legacy from years of French occupation, Morocco has the best wine industry in North Africa and wine drinking nowadays is quite widespread. Thibarine and boukha are favourite liqueurs made from figs.

MEAT

Meat has always been a comparative luxury in North Africa, so it is not served at every meal and is often "stretched" by combining with vegetables. Traditionally, mutton and lamb are the most widely used meats, but beef and veal are becoming popular. Lamb is prepared in a variety of ways. Legs and shoulders are roasted for special occasions, cubes of lamb are broiled on skewers and less tender

cuts of lamb and beef are marinated and cooked slowly. Ground lamb or beef is popular as a filling for savory pastries and for stuffing vegetables.

POULTRY AND GAME

A whole roasted chicken is a usual festive dish, and chicken pieces are frequently cooked in casseroles. Lean chicken breast meat is ideal for marinating to keep it moist, then broiling. Pheasant, duck, goose, quail and pigeon are frequently eaten and turkey is becoming more popular.

DAIRY PRODUCE

Traditionally, sheep and goats have been the main dairy animals of North Africa, but cows' milk is now produced throughout the area. Processed yogurt, cheese and samn (a strongly flavored ghee-type butter) are often eaten. Milk products and eggs form an essential part of breakfast, which will include yogurt and cheese, especially a salt preserved white cheese. Eggs are popular and are served hard-boiled, stuffed, fried, scrambled or in omelets. Hard-boiled eggs are often used to decorate stews, and are dyed for festive occasions.

FISH AND SHELLFISH

The waters of the North African coast are home to a wide range of fish and shellfish. Morocco is bordered by the Atlantic and the Mediterranean, providing fish from two different seas. Whole fried or broiled fish is particularly popular but there are also many recipes for stews and soups. Red and grey mullet are widely used, as are turbot, bass, sea bream, swordfish, tuna, sardines, monkfish as well as shellfish such as scallops, crabs, mussels, shrimp and lobster. Squid, cuttlefish and octopus are frequently fried, broiled and stewed.

VEGETABLES

Vegetables are treated with great respect and frequently feature as a dish in their own right in North African cuisine, rather than as an accompaniment, either stuffed or combined with other substantial ingredients. Zucchini, eggplants, bell peppers, cucumbers, tomatoes, onions, garlic, lettuce, artichokes, okra or bamia, small tender leaved spinach, beans, leeks and fennel all grow abundantly and are widely used in North African cooking.

FRUIT AND NUTS

A visit to any market will reveal the variety of brightly colored fruits that flourish in the area. Bananas, peaches, oranges, lemons, mangoes, melons, figs, watermelon, pomegranates, dates, grapes and apricots are all plentiful. Many fruits are dried and used in both sweet and savory dishes. Orange juice is used to flavor soups, sauces, cakes and pastries and lemon and lime juice is squeezed onto meat, fish or poultry before broiling.

Preserved lemons add a distinctive flavor to many dishes, and they are easy to make. You need 6 unwaxed, thin-skinned lemons. Scrub them well and soak in cold water for 2 days, changing the water once. Quarter the lemons from the top to within ½ inch of the bottom. Measure 4 oz. coarse salt and sprinkle some salt into the cut flesh and reshape the lemons. Place half the remaining salt in the bottom of a canning jar, then pack in the lemons. Add the remaining salt and press down on the lemons. Cover with freshly squeezed lemon juice and seal the jars. Keep for at least one month. Rinse thoroughly before using in recipes.

Olives and vines are also very important crops. Olives are served at nearly every meal and olive oil is an essential oil for frying, marinating, dressing and sauces. Grapes are used as dessert grapes and for wine making and the leaves are wrapped around a variety of fillings to make dolmades.

Nuts are grown throughout North Africa and are used in both sweet and savory dishes. Walnuts and hazelnuts are both popular, but almonds, pistachio nuts and pine nuts are particularly valued.

HERBS, SPICES AND FLAVORINGS

Herbs and spices are used, not only for their taste, but also for their medicinal and therapeutic value. A bunch of herbs is often placed on the dining table for guests to help themselves during the meal. The favorite herbs in North African cooking are flat leaved parsley and mint, but oregano, wild marjoram, thyme, cilantro and basil also feature heavily. Dried mint has a more concentrated flavor than the fresh herb and is often used in preference to fresh.

Every town has a spice street in the souk or market and spices have an important place in North African cooking. The most widely used are cinnamon, cumin, coriander, saffron, turmeric, ginger, black pepper, cayenne, paprika, allspice, aniseed, sesame seeds, caraway and cloves. **Tahini** is an oily paste made from crushed sesame seeds and is used in sauces and dips. **Ground sumac** is a less widely known spice which is used to add a sour flavor in marinades and salad dressings, or is rubbed onto meat, fish or chicken before broiling.

There are several spice blends which are essential to North African cooking. **Harissa** is a fiery chile sauce which is used as a table condiment and is stirred into soups and stews or added to the sauce for couscous. Every spice merchant has his own recipe of **Ras el Hanout**, which can contain as many as 20 different spices. The mixture is sold whole, then ground by the cook as required. **La Kama** is another simpler blend that contains only five spices – cinnamon, black peppercorns, ginger, turmeric and nutmeg. Used to flavor soups and stews, it is especially good with lamb. **Tabil** is specific to Tunisia. It literally means coriander, but usually refers to a blend of coriander seeds, caraway seeds, garlic and dried crushed chile. The ingredients are pounded together then dried before grinding. **Zahtar** is a mixture of ground sumac and powdered dried thyme combined with an equal quantity of toasted sesame seeds.

Other popular flavorings include rosewater and orange flower water, which only need to be used in small amounts to add fragrance and flavor to many sweet dishes. Pomegranates are used for flavoring in several different ways. The dried seeds have an astringent aroma and sweet-sour taste. They are often crushed and sprinkled on hummus, or added to fruit salads. Pomegranate syrup is frequently used and has an intense flavor.

PULSES AND GRAINS

Traditionally, pulses were dried for use during the winter months and they still feature very strongly in a wide variety of North African dishes, especially salads, soups, stews and bean purées or dips. All kinds of lentils are popular and chick-peas and beans, particularly fava beans, appear at most meals. Dried fava beans are particularly popular in Egypt where they are used to make the classic "ful medames."

Wheat is an important crop, and the variety grown in this area is a hard durum wheat, which is ideal for making bread. A wide range of leavened and unleavened bread is produced and is eaten with every meal, often being used as a scoop to pick up food. Many people still make their own bread, frequently cooking on an open fire or in a charcoal oven.

Wheat flour is also used for making the pastry which is used in the many sweet and savory pastry packages; these come in a wide variety of shapes – squares, triangles, cylinders and semicircles. Each country has its own variation on filo pastry. The warka pastry of Morocco is rarely made at home as it requires a high level of skill and is very time consuming. Tunisia's malsouqua pastry is made into pastries known as briks.

Wheat also provides the semolina for making couscous. Nowadays, much of the couscous sold is "instant" which is pre-prepared and only needs soaking briefly before steaming for a few minutes to warm it through. It is generally felt that the traditional couscous that requires more lengthy preparation is superior in texture and flavor. Unless stated otherwise, the recipes in this book use the instant variety, but if time allows, the regular couscous could be used instead.

Bulgar wheat is made of boiled grains of cracked wheat. It has a light nutty taste and can be used in similar ways to couscous. Secondary cereal crops include rice and corn.

EQUIPMENT

North African kitchens tend to be basic and cooking utensils and equipment are limited; a reflection of the elegant simplicity of most North African cooking. Ovens have only recently been introduced to home kitchens and it is more usual for dishes to be simmered on top of the heat than in the oven. The source of heat is often a charcoal brazier or mishmir, and if a dish requires a browned top an earthenware platter heaped with burning charcoal will be placed on it.

Essential pieces of equipment include a couscoussière for cooking meat, fish, poultry and vegetables. They are made of tin, aluminium, copper, stainless steel or even earthenware and consist of a bellied pot or gdra at the base with a steamer or kskas to fit on top. The steamer's perforated base allows the steam from whatever is cooking below to penetrate the couscous in the top. A cheesecloth-lined colander on top of a stock pot can be used as a substitute.

Most kitchens will contain several tagines – the glazed earthenware dishes with a conical earthenware cover. They are used for cooking stews of meat, poultry, fish or vegetables. Only a small amount of liquid is added to these dishes and the shape of the lid allows the steam in the dish to condense back into the food so that it does not dry out. Tagines are designed for use on a charcoal cooker and if they are used on gas or electric burners they must be placed on a heat diffuser. A tagine with a cast iron base that can be used on any type of stove is now available. The shallow base enables diners to help themselves. A conventional casserole can be used instead of a tagine but the food will have to be transferred to platters if you wish to eat with your fingers in the traditional manner.

Other pieces of equipment found in most kitchens include a gsaa or large round earthenware basin used for kneading bread dough and a midouna, which is a large flat basket used for separating the grains of couscous. There will also be a collection of skewers, sometimes in silver, for cooking brochettes, and there may be a damossa, which is a wide bellied pot with a slender neck for cooking over an outdoor fire. Most of the other cooking pots in the kitchen will be earthenware or tin-lined copper. There will also be copper, silver and brass serving trays, teapots, tea glasses and coffee pots.

HARIRA

4 tablespoons olive oil
1 large onion, finely chopped
2 cloves garlic, crushed
1 teaspoon turmeric
1 teaspoon ground ginger
1 teaspoon ground cumin
6¾ cups chicken or vegetable stock
8 oz. (1¼ cups) green lentils, washed
1 (14-oz.) can chopped tomatoes
1 (15-oz.) can chick-peas, drained
3 tablespoons chopped fresh cilantro
3 tablespoons chopped fresh parsley
Salt and freshly ground black pepper
Lemon juice, optional
Olive oil and Harissa (see page 46), to serve

In a large saucepan, heat half the oil. Add the onion and cook 10 minutes, until soft. Add the garlic, turmeric, ginger and cumin and cook a few more minutes. Stir in the stock and add the lentils and tomatoes. Bring to a boil, cover and simmer 20 minutes or until the lentils are soft. Stir in the chick-peas, remaining olive oil, cilantro, parsley, salt, pepper and lemon juice, if using, and simmer 5 more minutes.

To serve, pour some olive oil into a small bowl and spoon some harissa into another small bowl. Ladle the soup into heated bowls and place the olive oil and harissa on the table for people to help themselves.

Makes 6-8 servings.

Note: 4oz. dried chick-peas may be used instead of canned ones. They should be soaked overnight and simmered 1 hour or until soft, before adding with the lentils.

SPINACH SOUP

9 oz. young fresh spinach
¼ cup long grain rice
2 tablespoons olive oil
1 onion, finely chopped
2 cloves garlic, crushed
1 teaspoon ground coriander
4 scallions, finely chopped
4½ cups vegetable or chicken stock
Salt and freshly ground black pepper
2 cups (16 oz.) Greek yogurt
Grated lemon rind, to garnish

Remove any coarse stalks from the spinach. Wash the spinach in plenty of water and drain thoroughly. Cut into shreds.

Wash the rice in several changes of water and leave to drain. In a large saucepan, heat the oil. Add the onion and garlic and cook 10 minutes, until soft. Stir in the ground coriander and cook 2 more minutes. Stir in the scallions and the drained rice. Pour in the stock and season with salt and pepper.

Bring to a boil, cover and simmer gently 10 minutes then add the spinach and cook 5 minutes until the rice and spinach are cooked. The rice should not be too soft. Stir the yogurt into the soup. Heat without boiling and pour into warmed bowls. Serve, garnished with lemon rind.

Makes 6 servings.

—SQUASH SOUP & MINT PURÉE—

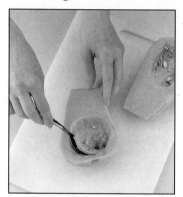

1 butternut squash, about 1 lb.
2 tablespoons butter
1 onion, finely chopped
1 clove garlic, crushed
½ teaspoon each ground turmeric and ground cumin
3¾ cups chicken or vegetable stock
Salt and freshly ground black pepper
Toasted cumin seeds, to garnish
MINT PURÉE
1 small bunch fresh mint
2 tablespoons olive oil
1 teaspoon lemon juice

Peel the squash, remove the seeds and roughly chop the flesh.

In a large saucepan, heat the butter. Add the chopped onion and cook gently 10 minutes until soft. Stir in the garlic, turmeric and cumin and cook, stirring, 2 more minutes. Add the pieces of squash and stock and season with salt and pepper. Bring to a boil then cover and simmer 20 minutes until the squash is soft.

Meanwhile, make the mint purée. In a mortar and pestle, pound the mint with a large pinch of salt. Add the olive oil and lemon juice and mix to a purée. In a blender or food processor, process the squash soup until smooth. Check the seasoning and pour into heated bowls. Add a spoonful of purée to each and garnish with toasted cumin seeds.

Makes 4-6 servings.

Note: If butternut squash is not available, other squashes such as pumpkin may be used.

──────── SEAFOOD SOUP ────────

1 lb. firm fish fillets
1 lb. mixed prepared raw shellfish, such as shrimp
in the shell, squid, scallops
1 recipe Chermoula (see page 42)
1 red bell pepper, seeded and chopped
12-16 mussels
Chopped fresh parsley, to serve
FISH STOCK
Fish trimmings such as bones, heads, shrimp shells etc.
2 onions, sliced
⅓ cup olive oil
8 black peppercorns
Handful mixed cilantro and parsley, including stalks
3 cloves garlic, sliced
4 tomatoes, roughly chopped
Salt

To make the stock, in a saucepan put the fish trimmings, onions, olive oil, peppercorns, cilantro, parsley, garlic, tomatoes and salt. Add 9 cups water and bring to a boil. Simmer gently, uncovered, for 45 minutes. Press the stock through a sieve into a clean pan. Cut the fish into cubes and place in a bowl with the shellfish. Add half the chermoula. Mix well to coat thoroughly, then cover the bowl and refrigerate 30 minutes.

Add the red bell pepper to the fish stock and simmer for 5 minutes until the pepper is tender. Add the fish and shellfish and simmer 3 to 4 minutes until the fish is cooked. Add the mussels and cook 2 more minutes or until they open. Discard any mussels that do not open. Adjust the seasoning and spoon into heated bowls. Serve with a little of the remaining chermoula in each bowl. Scatter the parsley over.

Makes 6 main meal servings or 8 first course servings.

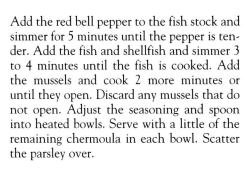

—LENTIL SOUP WITH ARUGULA—

2 tablespoons olive oil
1 onion, finely chopped
2 cloves garlic, crushed
1 teaspoon ground cumin
6¾ cups chicken or vegetable stock
7 oz. (1 cup) red lentils
8 oz. arugula
Salt and freshly ground black pepper
Olive oil, to serve

In a large saucepan, heat the olive oil. Add the onion and garlic and cook 10 minutes until soft.

Stir in the cumin and cook 2 more minutes. Add the stock and bring to a boil then stir in the lentils. Cover and simmer 20 minutes or until the lentils are soft, but not disintegrating.

Chop the arugula, including the stalks, very roughly and add to the soup. Season with salt and pepper, cover and simmer 2 more minutes. To serve, pour the soup into heated soup bowls and drizzle a little olive oil over.

Makes 6 servings.

— CUCUMBER & YOGURT SOUP —

1 large cucumber
2½ cups (20 oz.) Greek yogurt
2 cloves garlic, crushed
Finely grated rind of 1 lemon
2 tablespoons chopped fresh mint
Salt and freshly ground black pepper
Mint leaves, to garnish

Rinse the cucumber and trim the ends. Do not peel. Grate the cucumber into a bowl.

Stir in the yogurt, garlic, lemon rind and chopped mint. Season well with salt and pepper. Cover the bowl and chill 1 hour.

Stir in ⅔ cup iced water. Add more water if the soup seems a little thick. Adjust the seasoning then pour into chilled soup bowls. Garnish with mint leaves.

Makes 6 servings.

Variation: Cooked, peeled shrimp may be added to this soup.

BABA GANOUSH

2 small eggplants
1 clove garlic, crushed
4 tablespoons tahini
1 oz. (¼ cup) ground almonds
Juice of ½ lemon
½ teaspoon ground cumin
Salt and freshly ground black pepper
1 tablespoon chopped fresh mint leaves
2 tablespoons olive oil
Fresh mint leaves, to garnish
Selection of vegetables such as baby artichokes,
   radishes, sliced bell peppers, to serve

Place eggplants under a hot broiler, turning often, until black and blistered.

Remove the skins, chop the flesh roughly and leave to drain in a colander 10 minutes. Squeeze out as much liquid from the eggplants as possible and place the flesh in a food processor or blender. Add garlic, tahini, ground almonds, lemon juice, cumin, salt and pepper and process to a smooth paste.

Stir the chopped mint leaves into the dip. Spoon into a bowl and drizzle with olive oil. Scatter mint leaves on top. Place the bowl on a serving platter and serve with the vegetable selection.

Makes 6 servings.

BISSARA

1 lb. frozen fava beans
4 cloves garlic, crushed
3 scallions, roughly chopped
1 teaspoon ground cumin
2 tablespoons each chopped fresh mint, chopped
 fresh cilantro, and chopped fresh parsley
Salt
Pinch cayenne pepper
Juice of ½ lemon
Toasted Arab bread, olive oil and cayenne pepper, to
 serve

Boil the beans 5 minutes, or until tender.
Drain, reserving a little of the cooking liquid, and refresh in cold water. Drain again.

Slip the beans out of their skins and place in
a food processor or blender with the garlic.
Process to a rough purée then add the scallions, cumin, mint, cilantro, parsley, salt,
cayenne pepper and lemon juice. Process
again until thoroughly blended. Add enough
of the reserved cooking liquid to make a
spreading consistency.

To serve, spread the purée on the toasted
bread. Drizzle a little olive oil over and sprinkle with cayenne pepper. Cut into smaller
pieces, as desired.

Makes 6 to 8 servings.

Note: Bissara is traditionally made with
dried fava beans.

Variation: Add sufficient cooking liquid to
make a dipping consistency and serve with
raw vegetables.

—CARROT SALAD WITH PITA—

1 lb. carrots, peeled and thickly sliced
2 cloves garlic, crushed
¼ teaspoon cayenne pepper
½ teaspoon ground cumin
½ teaspoon ground allspice
½ teaspoon sugar
Juice of ½ lemon
Salt and freshly ground black pepper
¾ cup olive oil
4 pita breads
Fresh mint leaves, to garnish
ZAHTAR
2 oz. (½ cup) sesame seeds
1 oz. ground sumac
1 oz. ground dried thyme

Boil carrots 5 to 10 minutes until soft. Drain, refresh in cold water and drain again. Place in a food processor or blender with garlic, cayenne pepper, cumin, allspice, sugar, lemon juice, salt and pepper. Process until smooth; continue to process while trickling in 4 tablespoons of the olive oil. Check seasoning and transfer to a serving bowl. Cover and chill 2 hours. To make the zahtar, in a heavy skillet, dry roast sesame seeds over a medium heat, stirring, until lightly browned. Place in a bowl and leave to cool. Stir in sumac and thyme. Set aside.

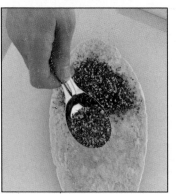

Split the pita breads in half. Drizzle the remaining olive oil over the cut sides of the bread and sprinkle 1 tablespoon of zahtar over each piece. Broil under a warm broiler until browned and crisp. When cool, break into rough pieces. Allow the carrot salad to come to room temperature. Garnish with mint leaves and serve with the pita toasts.

Makes 6 servings.

Note: Store the unused zahtar in a screw-top jar up to 3 months.

DUKKAH

4 oz. (1 cup) sesame seeds
2 oz. (⅓ cup) shelled, skinned hazelnuts
2 oz. coriander seeds
1 oz. ground cumin
1 teaspoon dried thyme
1 teaspoon salt
½ teaspoon freshly ground black pepper
Bread and olive oil, to serve

Heat a large heavy skillet over a medium heat. Add the sesame seeds and roast, stirring, until they are a light golden brown. Set aside to cool.

Add the hazelnuts to the pan and roast, stirring until lightly and evenly browned. Set aside to cool. Add the coriander seeds to the pan and roast until they begin to pop. Set aside to cool. Place the sesame seeds, hazelnuts, coriander seeds, cumin, thyme, salt and pepper in a food processor or blender and process to a coarse powder.

Transfer the dukkah to a serving bowl. To serve, dip a piece of bread into the olive oil and then into the dukkah mixture.

Makes 6 servings.

Note: Take care not to over-grind the nuts and seeds otherwise they will release their oils and form a paste. Dukkah can be made in large quantities and stored in an airtight container.

MARINATED OLIVES

4 oz. (¾ cup) black olives
4 oz. (¾ cup) green olives
1 preserved lemon (see page 10)
1 tablespoon coriander seeds
2 cloves garlic
3 dried red chiles
2 bay leaves
1 teaspoon green peppercorns in brine, drained
Olive oil

Make 2 or 3 cuts lengthwise in each olive. Place them in a bowl. Cut the peel from the preserved lemon into small pieces and add to the olives.

In a mortar and pestle, lightly crush the coriander seeds and add to the olives. Crush the garlic and add to the olives with the dried chiles, bay leaves and green peppercorns. Mix well.

Spoon the olives into a canning jar. Cover with olive oil and seal the jar tightly. Leave to marinate in a cool dry place 1 week, turning the jar occasionally. To serve, transfer to a serving bowl and serve as an appetizer with drinks or as part of a selection of mezzes.

Makes 6 servings.

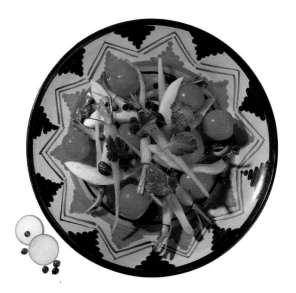

PICKLED VEGETABLES

8 oz. baby carrots
8 oz. radishes, trimmed
1 fennel bulb, sliced
2 teaspoons salt
4 tablespoons white wine vinegar
4 tablespoons sugar
1 tablespoon green peppercorns in brine, drained
1 tablespoon capers
Freshly ground black pepper
Cilantro leaves, to garnish

Peel and trim the carrots, leaving some green leaves attached at the top. Place in a bowl.

Add the radishes and fennel slices to the carrots in the bowl. Sprinkle the salt over and leave 2 hours. Drain the vegetables and rinse with cold water. Pat dry and return to the bowl.

In a saucepan, heat the vinegar and sugar, without boiling, until the sugar is dissolved. Pour the vinegar mixture over the vegetables and add the peppercorns, capers and pepper. Leave until cold then cover and refrigerate overnight. Serve the vegetables garnished with cilantro leaves.

Makes 6 servings.

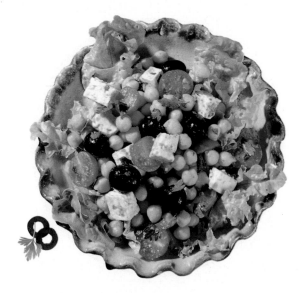

–CHICK-PEA, FETA & OLIVE SALAD–

2 (15-oz.) cans chick-peas, drained and rinsed
5 oz. feta cheese, cut into cubes
8 oz. cherry tomatoes
2 oz. pitted black olives
4 tablespoons flat leaf parsley
Salad greens, to serve
HARISSA DRESSING
5 tablespoons olive oil
1 tablespoon lemon juice
1 clove garlic, crushed
2 teaspoons Harissa (see page 46)
Salt

Place the chick-peas in a bowl and add the feta cheese cubes.

Unless the cherry tomatoes are very small, cut them in half and add to the chick-peas and feta cheese. Add the black olives and the flat leaf parsley.

To make the dressing, in a bowl whisk together the olive oil, lemon juice, garlic, harissa and salt. Pour the dressing over the chick-pea and tomato mixture and mix gently together. Arrange the salad greens on 6 plates and pile the salad on top. Serve immediately.

Makes 6 servings.

—GOAT CHEESE & FIG DRESSING—

⅓ cup couscous
1½ oz. pine nuts, finely chopped
Salt and freshly ground black pepper
1 tablespoon all-purpose flour
1 egg, beaten
3½ oz. soft goat cheeses, cut in half horizontally
Vegetable oil for frying
Salad greens, to serve
FIG DRESSING
6 tablespoons olive oil
3 tablespoons lemon juice
3 tablespoons orange juice
1 teaspoon cumin seeds, roughly crushed
2 teaspoons pink peppercorns, roughly crushed
2 ripe figs

Place the couscous in a bowl and just cover with boiling water. Leave to soak a few minutes. Fluff up the grains with a fork, then spread out on a baking sheet to dry for about 20 minutes. The grains should not dry completely. Place in a bowl, stir in the pine nuts and season with salt and pepper. Sift the flour onto a plate and pour the beaten egg into a shallow dish. Roll each cheese slice in the flour, then dip into the egg. Roll in the couscous to coat completely. Wrap each coated slice in plastic wrap and chill 1 hour.

To make the fig dressing, in a bowl, whisk together olive oil, lemon juice, orange juice, cumin seeds, pink peppercorns, salt and black pepper. Trim the fig stalks and cut the flesh into tiny dice. Stir into the vinaigrette and set aside. Arrange salad greens on 4 plates. In a skillet, heat about ½ inch oil. Add the cheese slices to the pan and fry, turning once, until the crust is lightly browned. Place a slice on each plated, drizzle with the dressing, and serve.

Makes 4 servings.

— SESAME-HERB LABNA BALLS —

2¼ cups (18 oz.) yogurt without stabilizers
A little cream or crème fraîche, optional
1 teaspoon salt
2 tablespoons sesame seeds
1 tablespoon chopped fresh parsley
1 tablespoon chopped fresh mint
Grape leaves, to decorate

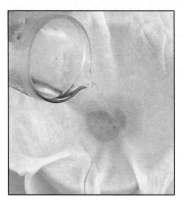

Place a nonreactive colander or sieve over a bowl. Place a large double square of cheesecloth in the colander and pour boiling water through, to scald it. Pour off the water.

Pour the yogurt into the cheesecloth square. Add the cream or crème fraîche, if using. Draw up the sides and corners of the cheesecloth and tie with string. Hang the cheesecloth bag over the bowl and leave in a cool place overnight. Tip the curds into a bowl and stir in the salt. Replace in the cheesecloth and hang over the bowl again for several more hours. Roll the cheese into balls and chill 1 hour.

Heat a skillet and add the sesame seeds. Heat until golden brown, stirring frequently. Transfer to a plate and leave to cool. On a plate, mix together the chopped parsley and mint. Roll half the balls in the sesame seeds and half in the herbs. Decorate with grape leaves and serve with pita bread.

Makes 4 servings.

Variation: Instead of rolling the mixture into balls, serve with olive oil drizzled over.

STUFFED ONION PETALS

1 large mild onion, peeled and quartered
Large pinch saffron threads
Salt and freshly ground black pepper
1 tablespoon olive oil
2 cloves garlic, crushed
1 teaspoon cumin seeds
8 oz. peeled new potatoes, cooked
2 tablespoons pine nuts
4 tablespoons Greek yogurt
1 tablespoon chopped fresh cilantro
Fresh cilantro leaves, to garnish

Separate the layers of the onion quarters to make "petals", reserving the central core.

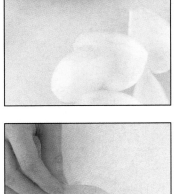

Add the saffron and onion petals to a large pan of boiling salted water. Boil 15 minutes, making sure they do not clump together, until thoroughly cooked and soft. Drain and dry on paper towels. Let cool. Finely chop the reserved onion core. Heat the oil in a skillet. Add the chopped onion, garlic and cumin seeds and cook gently 10 minutes or until the onion is soft. Let cool.

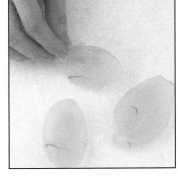

Cut the potatoes into tiny dice, place in a bowl and add the cooled onion mixture, pine nuts, yogurt, chopped cilantro, salt and pepper. Mix together gently. Place a teaspoon of the stuffing into each onion petal and gently press up the sides around the filling, forming canoe shapes with pointed ends. Arrange on a serving dish and garnish with cilantro leaves.

Makes 4 to 6 servings.

EGGPLANT STACKS

5 tablespoons olive oil
1 onion, finely chopped
1 clove garlic, crushed
1 red bell pepper, seeded and chopped
1 (14 oz.) can chopped tomatoes
6 sun-dried tomatoes in oil, drained and chopped
1 tablespoon raisins
½ teaspoon sugar
2 teaspoons balsamic vinegar
Salt and freshly ground black pepper
1 teaspoon dried mint
4 medium long-shaped eggplants
Fresh mint sprigs, to garnish

In a saucepan, heat 2 tablespoons of the olive oil. Add the onion and garlic and cook 10 minutes or until soft. Add the bell pepper, canned tomatoes, sun-dried tomatoes, raisins, sugar, vinegar, salt, pepper and mint. Simmer gently, uncovered, 20 minutes or until the mixture has thickened. Meanwhile, cut the eggplants into ¼-inch thick slices. Brush each slice on both sides with remaining olive oil.

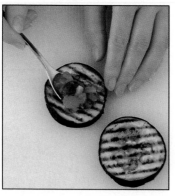

Heat a ridged cast iron broiler pan and broil the eggplant slices 3 to 4 minutes on each side until soft and browned. Keep hot while cooking the remaining slices. Spoon a little of the tomato mixture on an eggplant slice. Top with a second slice. Keep warm. Repeat with the remaining eggplant slices and tomato mixture. Serve garnished with mint sprigs.

Makes 6 servings.

──ROAST VEGETABLE CUPS──

2 medium eggplants, cut into ¾-inch cubes
4 medium zucchini, cut into ¾-inch cubes
1 red onion, chopped
2 cloves garlic, crushed
4 tablespoons olive oil
Juice of ½ lemon
2 teaspoons dried oregano
Salt and freshly ground black pepper
3 tablespoons butter, melted
6 sheets filo pastry, 16 x 12 inches
Strips of sun-dried tomatoes and toasted pine nuts,
  to garnish

Preheat the oven to 400F (205C). Place the eggplants, zucchini and onion in a large roasting pan. Add the garlic, olive oil, lemon juice, oregano, salt and pepper and mix well. Roast 30 minutes, stirring occasionally, until tender and slightly browned. Meanwhile, prepare the filo cups. Invert 12 individual ramekins on a baking sheet. Brush lightly with melted butter. Brush one sheet of pastry with melted butter and cut into 6 squares. Press 1 square, butter side up, over an upturned ramekin.

Repeat with a second square at an angle so that the points form petals. Repeat with a third square. Cover remaining ramekins in the same way. Remove vegetables from oven and keep warm. Reduce oven temperature to 375F (190C). Bake the cups 10 minutes until crisp and golden. Ease cups off the ramekins and place on a serving dish. Divide roasted vegetables among the cups. Garnish with sun-dried tomatoes and pine nuts and serve with salad.

Makes 12.

—TUNISIAN BRIK WITH TUNA—

1 tablespoon butter
1 small onion, finely chopped
1 clove garlic, crushed
1 (3½ oz.) can tuna in oil, drained
2 tablespoons chopped fresh parsley
Salt and freshly ground black pepper
2 sheets filo pastry, 16 x 12 inches
6 quail eggs
1 egg white, lightly beaten
Vegetable oil for frying
Lemon wedges, to garnish

Heat the butter in a skillet. Cook the onion and garlic gently 10 minutes, until soft. Transfer to a bowl; let cool.

Add the tuna, parsley, salt and pepper to the onion and mix well. Place one filo sheet on top of the other and cut into 6 squares. Place a spoonful of the tuna mixture on one triangular half of each filo square. Make a slight indentation in the mixture and carefully break a quail's egg into the hollow. Brush the edges of the pastry with beaten egg white and fold to make a triangle. Brush the joined edges again with egg white and fold over a small margin to make a stronger rim. Make 5 more triangular parcels or briks.

Heat 1 inch of oil in a large deep skillet. The oil should be hot, but not smoking. Slide the briks, in batches, into the hot oil. Spoon oil over the the top while frying. When the underside is lightly browned and crisp, turn and continue frying until the other side is brown. Drain on paper towels and keep warm while frying the remaining briks. Garnish with lemon wedges and serve hot, with salad greens.

Makes 6 servings.

- CHICK-PEA & CORIANDER CAKES -

2 (15-oz.) cans chick-peas, drained
2 cloves garlic, crushed
1 bunch scallions, chopped
2 teaspoons ground cumin
2 teaspoons ground coriander
1 fresh green chile, cored, seeded and finely chopped
2 tablespoons chopped fresh cilantro
1 small egg, beaten
2 tablespoons all-purpose flour, plus extra for dusting
Salt and freshly ground black pepper
Vegetable oil for shallow frying
Fresh cilantro, to garnish
CUCUMBER & YOGURT DIP
½ cucumber, peeled, seeded and diced
⅔ cup Greek yogurt
1 clove garlic, crushed

In a blender or food processor, process the
chick-peas until smooth. Add the garlic,
scallions, cumin and ground coriander.
Process again until well combined. Spoon
the mixture into a bowl and stir in the chile,
fresh cilantro, egg and flour. Mix well and
season with salt and pepper. If the mixture is
very soft add a little more flour. Chill about
30 minutes to firm the mixture.

To make cucumber and yogurt dip, place
cucumber in a colander, sprinkle with 1 teaspoon salt and leave to drain 30 minutes. Pat
dry with paper towels and place in a bowl.
Stir in the yogurt and garlic and season with
pepper. With floured hands, shape the
chick-pea mixture into 12 cakes. In a skillet,
heat the oil and fry the cakes 2 to 3 minutes
on each side, until crisp and golden. Drain
on paper towels. Garnish with fresh cilantro
and serve with the dip.

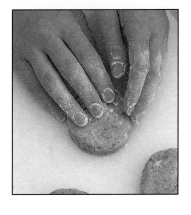

Makes 4 servings.

ZUCCHINI PANCAKES

2 zucchini, about 1lb. total weight
½ cup all-purpose flour
3 eggs
1 teaspoon chopped fresh mint
Salt and freshly ground black pepper
Vegetable oil for shallow frying
Mint sprigs, to garnish
RED BELL PEPPER SAUCE
1 tablespoon olive oil
1 small onion, chopped
1 clove garlic, crushed
2 red bell peppers, seeded and chopped
1 cup vegetable stock

To make the sauce, in a saucepan, heat oil, add onion and garlic and cook until soft. Add the red bell peppers and stock and simmer 10 minutes or until soft. Purée the mixture in a blender or food processor then press through a sieve. Set aside. Trim the zucchini and grate coarsely into a bowl. Sift the flour into a bowl and beat in the eggs to make a smooth batter. Stir in the mint and season with salt and pepper. Squeeze out as much liquid as possible from the grated zucchini and stir into the batter.

In a large heavy skillet, heat some oil. Fry tablespoons of mixture, in batches, about 4 minutes each side, until browned and cooked through. Keep warm while cooking the remainder. Reheat the red pepper sauce and serve with the zucchini pancakes, garnished with mint.

Makes 6 to 8 servings.

——LEEK & FAVA BEAN EGGAH——

3 tablespoons olive oil
2 medium leeks, trimmed, washed and thinly sliced
1 clove garlic, crushed
½ teaspoon sugar
Juice of ½ lemon
6 eggs
Salt and freshly ground black pepper
10 oz. fresh or frozen fava beans, cooked
CHERRY TOMATO SALSA
1 tablespoon lemon juice
¼ cup olive oil
¼ teaspoon cayenne pepper
1 tablespoon chopped fresh chives
8 oz. cherry tomatoes, halved
4 scallions, thinly sliced

Make the cherry tomato salsa. In a bowl, mix together the lemon juice, olive oil, cayenne, chives and salt. Add the tomatoes and scallions and mix well. Set the salsa aside. Heat 1 tablespoon of the oil in a skillet, add leeks and garlic and cook gently 10 to 15 minutes until leeks are soft and lightly colored. Stir in sugar and lemon juice and cook briskly to evaporate any liquid. In a large bowl, beat eggs lightly and season with salt and pepper. Stir in leeks and fava beans.

Heat remaining oil in a heavy 9-inch skillet. Pour in the egg mixture and cook, covered, over very low heat about 20 minutes until almost set, and the underside is browned. Place under a medium broiler 1 or 2 minutes to lightly brown and set the top. Cut into wedges and serve with the tomato salsa.

Makes 4 servings.

Note: This is equally good hot or cold, and can be served as a snack or a main course.

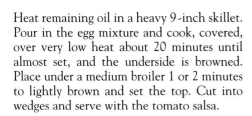

—HUMMUS & GRILLED CHICKEN—

2 boneless, skinless chicken breasts
Juice of ½ lemon
⅓ cup olive oil
Salt and freshly ground black pepper
2 teaspoons toasted sesame seeds
1 teaspoon ground cumin
½ teaspoon paprika
8 slices ciabatta-type bread
Lettuce leaves, to garnish
HUMMUS
1 (15-oz.) can chick-peas, drained
4 tablespoons tahini
4 tablespoons Greek yogurt
2 cloves garlic, crushed
1 tablespoons olive oil
Juice of 1 lemon

Place chicken breasts in a shallow dish. In a bowl, mix together lemon juice, 2 table-spoons of the olive oil, salt and pepper and pour over chicken. Cover and refrigerate 1 hour. To make the hummus, place chick-peas, tahini, yogurt, garlic, olive oil, lemon juice, salt and pepper in a blender or food processor and process to form a slightly grainy paste.

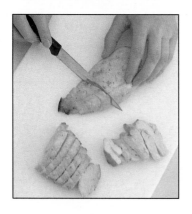

Broil the chicken breasts under a preheated broiler 15 minutes, turning once, until cooked through. Cut into slices and keep warm. Mix together the sesame seeds, cumin, paprika and salt. Drizzle the bread on both sides with olive oil and toast under the broiler. Spread some hummus on each piece of toast, top with chicken slices and sprinkle with sesame seed mixture. Drizzle with remaining olive oil and serve, garnished with salad leaves.

Makes 4 to 8 servings.

MOROCCAN LAMB ROLLS

1 tablespoon pine nuts
4 tablespoons olive oil
1 onion, finely chopped
12 oz. lean ground lamb
½ teaspoon ground cinnamon
1 tablespoon chopped fresh mint
Salt and freshly ground black pepper
6 sheets filo pastry, 16 x 12 inches
Fresh mint, to garnish
TAHINI & LEMON DIP
2 tablespoons tahini
Juice of 1 lemon
2 cloves garlic, crushed

In a skillet, heat pine nuts until golden. Remove from the pan and set aside.

In a skillet, heat 2 tablespoons of the oil. Add the onion and cook 10 minutes until soft. Stir in the lamb and cook, stirring, a few minutes until browned. Add the cinnamon, mint, pine nuts, salt and pepper. Cook a further 10 minutes then leave to cool. Preheat the oven to 350F (180C). Cut each sheet of filo pastry across into 3 strips. Brush the strips with the remaining oil.

Spread a spoonful of the lamb filling in a line on one end of each filo strip, leaving a small margin on either side. Roll over twice and fold the long sides over the edge, then continue rolling to make a tube. Place the rolls on a baking sheet. Bake 20 to 30 minutes until crisp and golden. Meanwhile, make the tahini and lemon dip. In a bowl, mix together the tahini, lemon juice and garlic. Garnish the lamb rolls with mint and serve with the dip.

Makes 18.

FISH COUSCOUS

1 tablespoon vegetable oil
2 onions, chopped
8 oz. baby carrots, trimmed
8 oz. baby turnips, quartered
2 celery stalks, cut into chunks
2½ cups fish stock
Salt and freshly ground black pepper
½ teaspoon saffron threads
1½ teaspoons tabil (see page 10)
8 oz. baby zucchini, trimmed
1 bunch scallions
8 oz. tomatoes, peeled and quartered
4 oz. shelled green peas
2¼ lbs. skinless cod fillet
1 lb. (2½ cups) couscous
Harissa (see page 46), to serve

In a large saucepan, heat the oil. Add the onions and cook gently 10 minutes until soft. Add the carrots, turnips, celery and stock. Season generously with salt and pepper and add the saffron and tabil. Bring to a boil, cover and simmer 10 minutes. Add the zucchini and simmer 10 minutes then add the scallions, tomatoes and peas.

Cut the fish into large pieces and place on top of the vegetables. Cover and simmer 10 minutes until the fish flakes easily when tested with a knife. Meanwhile, prepare couscous as directed on the package. To serve, pile couscous in a large heated serving dish. Arrange vegetables over couscous and place fish on top. Stir harissa, to taste, into broth and pour as much as desired over the couscous. Serve extra broth and harissa separately.

Makes 6 servings.

─SARDINES IN GRAPE LEAVES─

3 unwaxed thin-skinned lemons, quartered lengthwise
3 tablespoons sea salt
2 tablespoons sugar
12 large grape leaves in brine
12 fresh sardines, scaled and gutted
Lettuce leaves, to garnish
STUFFING
4 tablespoons chopped fresh cilantro
4 tablespoons chopped fresh parsley
2 cloves garlic, crushed
Salt and freshly ground black pepper
¼ cup olive oil

Preheat oven to 375F (190C). Place lemon quarters in an ovenproof dish with salt and sugar and mix well. Cover with foil. Bake 1 to 1½ hours until soft. Let cool. Place the grape leaves in a bowl and cover with cold water. Leave to soak one hour, changing the water twice. Drain and pat dry. Remove the backbone from the sardines by pressing down along the length of the backbone to flatten them. Pull out the backbone and wash and dry the fish.

To make the stuffing, in a bowl, mix together the cilantro, parsley, garlic, salt, pepper and olive oil. Stuff the fish with the herb mixture. Roll each fish up in a grape leaf. Place under a preheated broiler or on a grill and broil 3 to 5 minutes on each side until the grape leaves are crisp and the fish flakes easily when tested with a knife. Garnish with lettuce leaves, and serve with the roasted lemons.

Makes 4 to 6 servings.

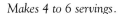

–FISH WITH COUSBAREIA SAUCE–

4 tomatoes
2 tablespoons olive oil
1 onion, chopped
1 clove garlic, crushed
4 oz. (¾ cup) hazelnuts, finely chopped
2 oz. pine nuts
3 tablespoons chopped fresh parsley
Salt and freshly ground black pepper
Fillets from 4 red mullet, skinned
Parsley sprigs, to garnish

Place the tomatoes in a bowl and cover with boiling water. Leave 1 minute then drain and cover with cold water.

Let stand 1 minute then peel the skins off the tomatoes. Remove the seeds and cut the flesh into dice. In a large skillet, heat the oil. Add the onion and garlic and cook 10 to 15 minutes until soft. Add the hazelnuts and pine nuts and fry 2 more minutes. Stir in the tomatoes and cook 3 or 4 minutes until soft. Add ⅔ cup water to cover, the parsley, salt and pepper and simmer 5 minutes.

Place the red mullet fillets in the pan and spoon some of the sauce over. Cover and simmer 10 to 15 minutes until the fish flakes easily when tested with a knife. Serve the fish fillets on heated plates with the sauce poured round. Garnish with parsley sprigs, and serve with lettuce leaves.

Makes 4 servings.

—STUFFED SEA BASS & SALAD—

1 clove garlic, crushed
Salt and freshly ground black pepper
3 teaspoons lime juice
1 teaspoon ground cumin
¼ teaspoon chile powder
1 tablespoon olive oil
3lbs. sea bass, cleaned and scaled
1 (8-oz.) bag mixed salad greens
STUFFING
Large pinch saffron threads
2 tablespoons olive oil
6 scallions, chopped
1 oz. (¼ cup) ready-to-eat dried apricots, chopped
1 oz. (½ cup) fresh breadcrumbs
2 oz. (½ cup) chopped walnuts
¼ teaspoon ground cardamom

In a small bowl, mix together the garlic, salt, 2 teaspoons of the lime juice, cumin, chile powder and 1 tablespoon olive oil. Make several slashes in the skin of the fish and rub the marinade in well. Cover and leave in the refrigerator 1 hour. To make the stuffing, place the saffron in a small bowl with 1 tablespoon hot water. In a saucepan, heat 2 tablespoons oil. Add scallions and cook a few minutes until soft. Stir in apricots, breadcrumbs, walnuts, salt, pepper, cardamom and soaked saffron. Cook 1 minute then leave to cool.

Preheat oven to 350F (180C). Place the fish on a sheet of well oiled foil and fill the cavity with stuffing. Draw foil up to make a parcel. Place on a large baking sheet and bake 40 to 50 minutes until fish flakes easily when tested with a knife. To serve, cut into 4 fillets; arrange on 4 heated plates and keep warm. Heat the cooking juices in a pan and add the salad greens. Stir briefly until just wilted then add remaining lime juice; serve with the fish, and with a rice pilaf.

Makes 4 servings.

—FISH TAGINE WITH TOMATOES—

8 plum tomatoes, cut in half lengthwise
2 teaspoons sugar
Salt and freshly ground black pepper
2 tablespoons olive oil
1 bream weighing about 3 lbs., cleaned
1 recipe Chermoula (see page 42)
1 carrot, cut into matchsticks
2 celery stalks, cut into matchsticks
Peel of ½ preserved lemon (see page 10), cut into
  strips
Fresh parsley, to garnish

Preheat the oven to 475F (240C). Place the tomatoes in an ovenproof dish, cut side up. Sprinkle with sugar, salt and pepper.

Drizzle the tomatoes with the olive oil and roast in the oven 30 to 40 minutes until soft and slightly charred. Rub the fish, inside and out, with the chermoula. Place in a dish and leave in a cool place 30 minutes. Arrange the carrot and celery in the bottom of a tagine or ovenproof dish. Place the fish on top of the carrot and celery. Add any remaining chermoula and arrange the tomatoes and lemon peel round the sides.

Reduce the oven temperature to 400F (205C). Cover the dish with a lid or foil and bake in the oven 30 minutes. Remove the foil and spoon any juices over the fish. Return to the oven, uncovered, and cook a further 10 minutes, or until the fish flakes easily when tested with a knife, and most of the liquid has evaporated. Serve, garnished with parsley.

Makes 4 servings.

—SALMON & COUSCOUS CAKES—

⅔ cup couscous
8 oz. salmon fillet, skinned and boned
½ bunch scallions, chopped
1½ teaspoons cumin seeds, toasted and ground
2 teaspoons lemon juice
2 tablespoons chopped fresh cilantro
1 egg, beaten
3 tablespoons Greek yogurt
2 tablespoons vegetable oil
YELLOW TOMATO & PEPPER SALSA
1 orange bell pepper, seeded and quartered
4 yellow tomatoes, cut in quarters and seeded
½ bunch scallions, chopped
Juice of ½ lemon
4 tablespoons chopped fresh cilantro
Salt and freshly ground black pepper

To make the salsa, broil the bell pepper quarters, skin side up, 5 minutes until skin blisters and chars. Place in a plastic bag until cool enough to handle, then remove skin. Cut the tomatoes and bell pepper into fine dice and place in a bowl with the scallions, lemon juice, cilantro, salt and pepper. Stir salsa and chill until ready to serve. Place couscous in a bowl, add ¾ cup hot water and leave 10 to 15 minutes until water is absorbed.

Put 1½ inches water in a frying pan; season with salt and bring to a simmer. Add salmon and poach gently 5 minutes until fish flakes easily when tested with a knife. Drain and cool, then flake into the couscous. Stir in scallions, cumin, lemon juice, cilantro, egg, yogurt, salt and pepper. Form into 8 cakes and chill 30 minutes. In a skillet, heat the oil and fry the cakes 5 minutes on each side or until brown. Serve with the salsa and with salad leaves.

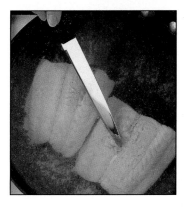

Makes 4 servings.

SWORDFISH KEBABS

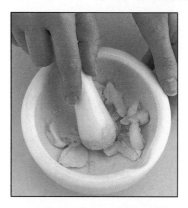

1½ lbs. skinless boneless swordfish steaks
CHERMOULA
4 cloves garlic, peeled
1 teaspoon salt
Juice of 2 lemons
1 tablespoon ground cumin
2 teaspoons paprika
1 fresh red chile, cored, seeded and roughly chopped
¼ cup lightly packed fresh cilantro
¼ cup lightly packed fresh parsley
¼ cup olive oil

To make the chermoula, in a mortar and pestle, crush the garlic with the salt. Place in a blender or food processor.

Add the lemon juice to the food processor with the cumin, paprika, red chile, cilantro and parsley. Process briefly then gradually add the olive oil and process to a coarse purée. Transfer to a bowl. Cut the swordfish into 1 inch cubes and add to the chermoula mixture. Mix well to coat, cover and refrigerate 1 hour.

Thread the fish onto skewers and place on a rack over a broiler pan. Spoon the marinade over the fish. Broil under a preheated broiler, close to the heat, 3 to 4 minutes on each side, until the fish is lightly browned and flakes easily when tested with a knife. Serve with Tomato, Olive & Caper Salad (see page 83) and warm pita bread.

Makes 4 servings.

Variation: Fish such as monkfish, or raw tiger shrimp may be used this recipe.

—MOROCCAN SEAFOOD PILAF—

1½ lbs. mixed fresh shellfish, e.g., squid, shrimp and
   scallops, cleaned
8 oz. skinless cod fillet, cut into bite sized pieces
1 recipe Chermoula (see opposite)
1½ lbs. mussels in their shells
2 tablespoons vegetable oil
2 celery stalks, sliced
2 red bell peppers, seeded and chopped
1 onion, chopped
1½ cups long grain rice
2½ cups fish stock
1 (14-oz.) can chopped tomatoes
Salt and freshly ground black pepper
Cilantro sprigs and lemon slices, to garnish

Cut the squid into ¼-inch rings, peel the
shrimp and halve the scallops. Place the
shellfish in a bowl with the cod, add the
chermoula and mix well. Cover and refrigerate 1 hour. Scrub the mussels, discarding any
open ones; cover and refrigerate. Heat the
oil in a large sauté pan. Add the celery and
peppers and fry 3 minutes, then remove and
set aside. Add the onion and cook 10 minutes until soft. Stir in the rice then add the
stock. Drain the fish and add the marinade
to the pan with the tomatoes, salt and
black pepper.

Bring to a boil, cover and simmer gently 30
minutes, stirring occasionally, until the rice
is cooked and the liquid is almost absorbed.
Add more stock, if necessary. Return the celery and peppers to the pan. Place the fish
and the mussels on top. Cover and simmer
10 minutes, or until the fish is cooked and
the mussels have opened. Discard any
unopened mussels. Let stand, covered, 10
minutes. Serve, garnished with cilantro and
lemon.

Makes 6 to 8 servings.

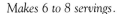

MOROCCAN SHRIMP

1 lb. raw peeled tiger shrimp
2 cloves garlic, crushed
1 teaspoon paprika
1 teaspoon ground cumin
½ teaspoon ground coriander
¼ teaspoon cayenne pepper
2 tablespoons olive oil
½ bunch scallions, finely sliced
2 tablespoons chopped fresh cilantro
AVOCADO & MELON SALSA
1 ripe avocado
Juice of 1 lime
8 oz. melon, seeded and cut into small dice
½ bunch scallions, finely chopped
1 fresh red chile, cored, seeded and finely chopped
Salt

To make the salsa, cut the avocado in half, remove the seed and peel off the skin. Dice the flesh finely and place in a bowl. Add the lime juice and mix well. Add the diced melon, scallions, chile and salt to taste. Cover and let stand 30 minutes.

If necessary, remove the heads and tails from the shrimp and devein. Rinse and pat dry with paper towels. In a bowl, mix together the garlic, salt, paprika, cumin, ground coriander and cayenne. Add the shrimp and mix well. In a large skillet, heat the oil. Add the shrimp and scallions and stir-fry 5 minutes or until the shrimp are pink and cooked through. Stir in the chopped cilantro. Serve with the salsa and with rice.

Makes 4 servings.

—SQUID WITH SAFFRON SAUCE—

1 lb. small squid
1 tablespoon vegetable oil
1 fennel bulb, very thinly sliced
2 tablespoons chopped fresh parsley
2 tablespoons chopped sun-dried tomatoes
Juice of ½ lemon
SAFFRON SAUCE
⅔ cup fish stock
4 saffron threads
⅔ cup mayonnaise
Lemon juice, to taste

To make the saffron sauce, boil the fish stock until reduced to 1 tablespoon. Add the saffron threads. Let cool.

Strain stock into a bowl and stir in mayonnaise. Season with salt, pepper and lemon juice. Clean the squid. Pull on tentacles; cut off just above the head, discarding head and intestinal sac. Slip quill-like transparent bone out of body. Rinse body inside and out, pulling away pink outer membrane. Dry on paper towels. Cut body into ¼-inch rings and cut the tentacles into small pieces.

In a skillet, heat the oil. Add the squid and sauté a minute or until it becomes opaque. Season with salt and pepper. Drain and set aside to cool. In a serving bowl, arrange the fennel, parsley and sun-dried tomatoes. Add the squid and pour the lemon juice over. Serve with the saffron sauce.

Makes 4 servings.

—SHRIMP & COUSCOUS SALAD—

5 tablespoons olive oil
2 shallots, finely chopped
1½ cups chicken stock
4 oz. shelled green peas
8 oz. (1 cup) couscous
2 teaspoons lemon juice
Salt and freshly ground black pepper
12 oz. cooked shrimp
Fresh mint, to garnish
HARISSA
12 dried red chiles
1 tablespoon coriander seeds
2 teaspoons cumin seeds
2 cloves garlic, peeled
½ teaspoon salt
4-6 tablespoons olive oil

To make the harissa, discard the stems and seeds from the chiles, then place in a bowl and cover with boiling water. Leave to soak 30 minutes until softened. In a heavy skillet, heat the coriander and cumin seeds until they smell aromatic. Grind to a powder in a grinder. Drain the chiles and place in a blender with the garlic, coriander mixture and salt. Blend together, trickling in the olive oil until the sauce has a mayonnaise-like consistency. In a pan, heat 2 tablespoons of the oil. Fry the shallots 10 minutes until soft.

Add 1 to 2 teaspoons of harissa, the stock and peas. Bring to a boil. Remove from the heat and stir in the couscous. Leave 10 minutes, until the stock is absorbed. Transfer to a shallow dish and let cool. In a bowl, whisk the lemon juice, remaining oil, salt and pepper. Stir into couscous with the shrimp. Serve warm, garnished with mint.

Makes 4 servings.

Note: To store the harissa, transfer to a screw-top jar and pour olive oil over the top.

CHICKEN TAGINE

2 lemons
2 tablespoons vegetable oil, plus oil for frying
1 onion, chopped
1 (3¼-3½ lbs.) chicken, cut into pieces
1 teaspoon ground cumin
1 teaspoon ground paprika
1 teaspoon ground ginger
Large pinch saffron threads, crushed
1 cinnamon stick
Salt and freshly ground black pepper
⅓ cup pitted green olives
Peel from 1 preserved lemon (see page 10), cut into
    strips
2 tablespoons chopped fresh cilantro
1 tablespoon chopped fresh parsley
Harissa (see page 46), to serve

With a zester, remove rind from the lemons and place in a bowl. Squeeze the juice over and set aside. In a Dutch oven, heat the oil. Add the onion and cook 10 minutes until soft. Remove the onion and add the chicken. Cook until browned all over. Stir in the cumin, paprika, ginger, saffron and cinnamon stick. Cook 1 minute then return the onions to the pan. Pour in 1 cup water. Season with salt and pepper and bring to a boil. Cover and simmer gently 45 minutes.

Stir in the olives, preserved lemon, cilantro and parsley and cook a further 10 to 15 minutes until the chicken is cooked. Meanwhile, drain the lemon rind and pat dry with paper towel. In a small saucepan, heat ½ inch oil. Add the rind, which will crisp almost immediately. Quickly drain off the oil through a sieve. Serve the chicken and sauce with the fried lemon rind scattered over. Serve with bread, and with the harissa served separately.

Makes 6 servings.

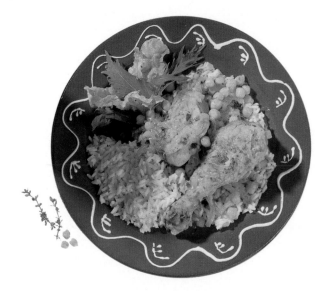

—SAFFRON CHICKEN CASSEROLE—

¾ cup dried chick-peas
½ teaspoon paprika
½ teaspoon each ground cumin and ground coriander
Salt and freshly ground black pepper
4½ lbs. chicken pieces
½ cup butter
1 tablespoon vegetable oil
2 large mild onions, thinly sliced
½ teaspoon saffron threads
4½ cups chicken stock
1 sprig thyme
4 tablespoons chopped fresh parsley
1¼ cups rice, to serve

Place chick-peas in a bowl. Cover with cold water and leave overnight to soak.

Drain the chick-peas and place in a saucepan, cover with water and bring to a boil. Boil 1 hour. In a bowl, mix together the paprika, cumin, coriander, salt and pepper. Toss the chicken pieces in the mixture. Heat the butter and oil in a large Dutch oven. Add the chicken pieces and sauté until browned. Transfer to a plate. Add the onions to the pan and cook 10 minutes until soft. Return the chicken pieces to the pan and add the chick-peas. Add the saffron threads to the stock.

Pour over enough stock to cover the chicken and bring to a boil. Add the thyme. Cover and simmer gently about 1 hour or until the chicken is tender. Stir in the chopped parsley and check the seasoning. Meanwhile, cook the rice in boiling salted water. To serve, drain the rice and arrange half of it a heated serving dish. Place the chicken and onions on top and pour over as much saffron sauce as desired. Add the remaining rice and serve with salad.

Makes 6 servings.

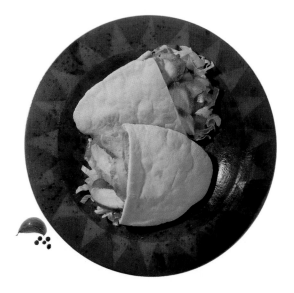

—MOROCCAN CHICKEN IN PITA—

½ cup Greek yogurt
2 teaspoons Harissa (see page 46)
2 teaspoons each ground cumin and ground coriander
2 cloves garlic, crushed
1 tablespoon olive oil
Salt and freshly ground black pepper
4 boneless, skinless chicken breasts
Pita bread, shredded lettuce and chopped tomatoes,
   to serve

In a bowl, mix together the yogurt, harissa, cumin, coriander, garlic, olive oil, salt and pepper. Spread over the chicken breasts and place in a dish. Cover the dish and place in the refrigerator 2 hours.

Preheat the oven to 200C (400F). Place the chicken breasts on a rack in a roasting pan and cook in the oven 25 minutes until browned and the juices run clear when pierced with a knife. Place the pita bread in the oven the last 5 minutes of cooking, to warm through.

To serve, cut the chicken into thin slices. Cut the pita bread in half and open to form pockets; fill the pockets with the sliced chicken, shredded lettuce and chopped tomatoes.

Makes 4 to 6 servings.

—TUNISIAN SPICED POUSSIN—

2 poussins
2 tablespoons butter
2 teaspoons paprika
2 teaspoons each honey and tomato paste
4 tablespoons lemon juice
⅔ cup chicken stock
1 teaspoon Harissa (see page 46)
STUFFING
2 tablespoons butter
1 onion, chopped
2 cloves garlic, crushed
1 teaspoon each ground cinnamon and ground cumin
1 oz. blanched almonds, finely chopped
6 oz. mixed ready-to-eat dried fruit, chopped
Salt and freshly ground black pepper

To make the stuffing, melt the butter in a saucepan. Add the onion and garlic and cook gently 10 minutes until soft. Add the cinnamon and cumin and cook, stirring, 2 minutes. Add the almonds and fruit, season with salt and pepper and cook 2 minutes. Let cool. Preheat the oven to 400F (200C). Stuff the neck end of the poussins with the stuffing. Set aside any excess. In a small saucepan, melt the butter with the paprika; brush over the poussins. Place in a roasting pan and roast 45 to 60 minutes, basting occasionally, until cooked.

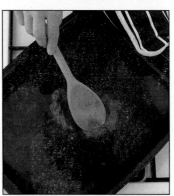

Transfer the poussins to a carving board. Pour any excess fat from the roasting pan. Stir the honey, tomato paste, lemon juice, stock and harissa into the juices in the pan. Add salt to taste. bring to a boil and simmer 2 minutes. Reheat any excess stuffing. Serve the poussins with the stuffing and sauce, and with parsley rice.

Makes 4 servings.

—DUCK TAGINE WITH PEARS—

1 tablespoon olive oil
3 duck breasts, about 2¼ lbs. total weight
4 onions, thinly sliced
3 cloves garlic, crushed
1 teaspoon sugar
2 teaspoons ground cinnamon
½ teaspoon saffron threads
1¼ cups chicken stock
Salt and freshly ground black pepper
4 oz. (¾ cup) ready-to-eat dried pears
3 tablespoons chopped fresh cilantro

Heat the oil in a large nonstick skillet. Add the duck, skin side up, and cook 1 to 2 minutes until lightly browned.

Turn the duck breasts and cook over low heat until the skin is brown and crisp. Remove and drain on paper towels. Pour off all but 3 tablespoons of fat. Add the onions and cook 15 minutes until completely soft. Slice the duck breasts crosswise into ½-inch slices. Place the onion and duck in a Dutch oven.

Stir in the garlic, sugar, cinnamon, saffron and stock. Season with salt and pepper. Cover and simmer gently 30 minutes. Cut the pears into pieces, add to the pan, cover and cook gently a further 30 minutes. Stir in the cilantro and serve with couscous.

Makes 6 servings.

BISTILLA

1 carrot, coarsely chopped
2 onions, 1 coarsely chopped, 1 finely chopped
2 pigeons
1 bay leaf
6 peppercorns
7 tablespoons butter
2 oz. (⅓ cup) blanched almonds, finely chopped
2 teaspoons sugar
½ teaspoon ground cinnamon
3 tablespoons chopped fresh parsley
4 eggs, lightly beaten
Salt and freshly ground black pepper
12 sheets filo pastry, 16 x 12 inches
Powdered sugar and ground cinnamon, to decorate

Place the carrot and coarsely chopped onion in a Dutch oven with the pigeons, bay leaf and peppercorns. Add enough water to cover. Bring to a boil, cover and simmer gently 45 to 60 minutes until the pigeons are very tender. Remove from the pan and set aside to cool. Strain the stock and reserve, discarding the vegetables. When the pigeons are cool enough to handle, cut the breasts away from the carcass. Remove the skin and cut the meat into small pieces. Set the pigeon meat aside.

Melt 1 tablespoon of the butter in a small skillet. Add the almonds and cook, stirring, 1 minute, or until light golden. Transfer to a bowl and cool. Stir in the sugar and cinnamon. Place the finely chopped onion in a saucepan with the parsley and ⅔ cup of the reserved stock. Bring to a boil, cover and simmer 15 minutes or until the onion is soft. Remove the lid and boil until the liquid has evaporated. Set aside to cool.

Whisk 2 tablespoons of the reserved stock into the lightly beaten eggs. Season with salt and pepper. Melt 2 tablespoons of the butter in a saucepan. Add the egg mixture and stir over a gentle heat until just set but still creamy. Preheat the oven to 350F (180C).

In a small saucepan, melt the remaining butter. Unwrap the filo sheets and keep loosely covered with plastic wrap until required. Cut 2 sheets of filo crosswise in half. Brush one half-sheet with melted butter. Place a second half-sheet on top and brush with butter. Repeat with the remaining two half-sheets. Press the buttered filo sheets into a 4-inch loose-bottomed flan pan allowing the excess to overhang the edge. Repeat with 5 more flan pans. Divide the egg mixture between the 6 flan pans. Cover with a layer of onion mixture, then almond mixture.

Arrange the pigeon meat on top and sprinkle 1 teaspoon of reserved stock over each pie. Trim the corners of the overhanging pastry then fold the pastry over the top of the pies, pressing down firmly. Brush each pie with melted butter. Bake in the oven 30 minutes until golden and crisp. Serve, sprinkled with powdered sugar and ground cinnamon, with a mixed salad.

Makes 6 servings.

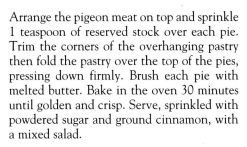

—QUAIL WITH GRAPES—

2 inches ginger root, peeled and finely chopped
8 quail
¼ cup butter
Salt and freshly ground black pepper
6 oz. seedless white grapes, halved
1 cup unsweetened white grape juice
1 teaspoon cornstarch
Fresh flat leaf parsley, to garnish

Preheat the oven to 425F (220C). Place some chopped ginger inside each quail. In a roasting dish, melt the butter. Add the quail and cook, turning, in the butter until browned all over. Season with salt and pepper.

Roast in the oven 20 minutes, basting occasionally, until the quail are browned and cooked through. Tilt the quail to let the juices run back into the pan. Transfer to a heated serving dish and keep warm.

Pour any fat from the roasting pan. Add the grapes and grape juice and place over the heat. Simmer a few minutes, scraping up the sediment, until the grapes are warm. In a bowl, blend the cornstarch with a little cold water and stir into the sauce. Simmer until thickened. Season with salt and pepper. Arrange the grapes around the quail and pour the sauce around. Serve with bulgar wheat or rice, garnished with flat leaf parsley.

Makes 4 servings.

GRILLED QUAIL & ARAB SALAD

8 quail
⅓ cup olive oil
Juice of 2 lemons
4 cloves garlic, crushed
Salt and freshly ground black pepper
2 tablespoons chopped fresh parsley
ARAB SALAD
1 teaspoon Harissa (see page 46)
5 tablespoons olive oil
2 tablespoons lemon juice
8 oz. cherry tomatoes, halved
1 small or ½ large cucumber, cut into cubes
1 bunch scallions, chopped
1 bunch watercress, washed and dried

With a pair of kitchen scissors, cut the quail down the backbone, turn them over and press down on the breastbone to flatten them out. Pat dry with paper towels. Pass two skewers through each quail. Place them in a glass dish. In a bowl, mix together the olive oil, lemon juice, garlic, salt and pepper and parsley. Pour over the quail. Cover and marinate in the refrigerator 4 to 6 hours.

To make the salad, in a bowl, mix together the harissa, olive oil, lemon juice, salt and pepper. Add the tomatoes, cucumber, scallions, and watercress. Mix lightly. Remove the quail from the marinade and place on the broiler rack. Broil under a preheated broiler 10 to 15 minutes, turning during cooking and brushing with the marinade. Serve with the salad.

Makes 4 servings.

──GUINEA FOWL IN BEETS──

1 lb. uncooked beets
1 onion, chopped
1¾ cups chicken stock
3 tablespoons butter
1 teaspoon ground cumin
½ teaspoon each ground allspice and ground cinnamon
1 guinea fowl, quartered
Salt and freshly ground black pepper
1 teaspoon cornstarch
4 tablespoons plain yogurt
Chopped fresh mint, to garnish

Place the beets in a pan of boiling water. Cover and simmer 30 to 60 minutes until tender. Drain.

Preheat the oven to 325F (170C). As soon as the beets are cool enough to handle, remove the skin. Cut the beets into chunks and place in a blender or food processor with the onion and chicken stock. Blend until completely smooth. In a Dutch oven, melt the butter. Add the cumin, allspice and cinnamon and cook 1 minute. Add the guinea fowl portions and cook until lightly browned.

Stir in the beet purée and season with salt and pepper. Heat to simmering point then cover and cook in the oven 1 hour or until the guinea fowl is very tender. Place the guinea fowl on a heated serving plate. Blend the cornstarch with a little cold water and pour into the sauce. bring to a boil and simmer 1 minute until slightly thickened. Pour the sauce over the guinea fowl; drizzle the yogurt over sauce and sprinkle with chopped mint. Serve with rice.

Makes 4 servings.

–MEATBALLS IN TOMATO SAUCE–

1 lb. lean ground beef
1 medium onion, grated
1 clove garlic, crushed
2 tablespoons fresh breadcrumbs
1 tablespoon chopped fresh parsley
1 tablespoon chopped fresh mint
½ teaspoon each ground cinnamon and ground coriander
Salt and freshly ground black pepper
Flour for dusting
2 tablespoons vegetable oil
TOMATO SAUCE
1 tablespoon olive oil
1 onion, finely chopped
1 clove garlic, crushed
1 (14-oz.) can chopped tomatoes
1 teaspoon sugar

To make the sauce, heat the olive oil in a saucepan. Add the onion and garlic and cook 10 minutes until soft. Add the tomatoes, sugar, salt and pepper. Simmer 5 minutes. In a blender or food processor, process the sauce until fairly smooth. Return to the saucepan and set aside.

In a large bowl, mix together the beef, onion, garlic, breadcrumbs, parsley, mint, cinnamon, coriander, salt and pepper. On a floured board, roll the mixture into small balls. In a skillet, heat the vegetable oil and fry the meatballs until browned all over and firm. Add to the tomato sauce and simmer 20 minutes until tender. Serve with rice garnished with mint.

Makes 4 servings.

MOROCCAN BROCHETTES

1 onion, roughly chopped
2 cloves garlic, roughly chopped
1 fresh red chile, seeded and cut into strips
1½ lbs. ground beef
4 tablespoons chopped fresh parsley
½ teaspoon dried oregano
1 teaspoon each paprika and ground cumin
1 teaspoon salt
½ teaspoon freshly ground black pepper
Yogurt and chopped scallions, to serve

Place the onion, garlic and chile in a food processor and process briefly. Add the ground beef, parsley, oregano, paprika, cumin, salt and pepper and blend to a paste.

Transfer the mixture to a bowl, cover and refrigerate 30 minutes. With damp hands, take an egg-sized piece of the mixture and press it into a long sausage shape on a skewer. (Skewers made from rosemary twigs may be used to add extra fragrance.)

Broil the brochettes under the broiler or on a grill, turning frequently, 6 to 7 minutes, until well browned on the outside but still moist inside. To serve, spoon yogurt over the brochettes and sprinkle with chopped scallions. Serve with salad and pita bread.

Makes 6 servings.

——BEEF TAGINE WITH PRUNES——

8 oz. (1¼ cups) pitted prunes
1 teaspoon ground ginger
1 tablespoon ground coriander
Pinch saffron threads
Salt and freshly ground black pepper
3 tablespoons olive oil
2¾ lbs. stew beef cubes
2 onions, sliced
2 cloves garlic, crushed
Chicken stock or water
1 cinnamon stick
1 tablespoon honey
1 teaspoon Harissa (see page 46)
1 tablespoon sesame seeds
3 tablespoons chopped fresh parsley
1 teaspoon orange flower water, to serve

Place the prunes in a bowl and cover with
boiling water. Let soak 2 hours. In a large
bowl, mix together the ginger, coriander,
saffron, salt, pepper and 2 tablespoons of the
oil. Add the beef and mix well, rubbing the
spices into the meat with your fingers.
Transfer to a tagine or Dutch oven. In a
large skillet, heat the remaining oil. Add
the onions and garlic and cook 10 minutes
until soft. Add to the spiced beef, then pour
in enough stock or water to barely cover the
meat. Add the cinnamon stick.

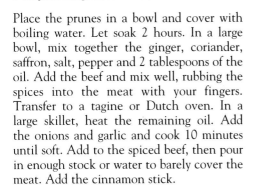

Cover the tagine and simmer gently 2 hours
until the beef is tender. Check from time to
time and add more liquid, if necessary.
Drain the prunes and add to the pan; simmer 20 minutes longer. Stir in the honey
and harissa and cook a further 15 minutes.
Dry fry the sesame seeds in a skillet until
lightly browned. To serve, stir in the parsley, sprinkle with orange flower water and
scatter the sesame seeds on top. Serve with
couscous.

Makes 6 servings.

–LAMB BURGERS & MINT RELISH–

1 lb. lean ground lamb
1 small onion, finely chopped
1 clove garlic, crushed
1 teaspoon each ground cumin and ground coriander
1 teaspoon Harissa (see page 46)
1 tablespoon chopped fresh parsley
Olive oil for brushing
Pita bread and salad, to serve
MINT RELISH
¾ cup lightly packed fresh mint
¼ cup lightly packed fresh cilantro
1 clove garlic, crushed
2 tablespoons lime juice
Salt and freshly ground black pepper
1 teaspoon sugar
2 tablespoons olive oil

To make the mint relish, reserve 4 sprigs of mint for garnish. Place the mint, cilantro, garlic, lime juice, salt, pepper, sugar and half the olive oil in a blender or food processor and process 1 minute; scrape down the sides of the bowl and process again to a paste. Transfer to a bowl and pour the remaining oil on top to prevent the paste discoloring.

Mix together the lamb, onion, garlic, cumin, coriander, harissa, parsley and salt until well combined. Shape into four burgers. Heat a ridged broiler pan. Brush the burgers with olive oil and cook 5 minutes on each side for well done. To serve, split the pita breads, place some salad on the bottom and then the burgers. Put a spoonful of the mint relish on each burger and garnish with the reserved mint leaves.

Makes 4 servings.

——LAMB KEBABS WITH SALSA——

2 cloves garlic, crushed
4 tablespoons lemon juice
2 tablespoons olive oil
1 dried red chile, crushed
1 teaspoon ground cumin
1 teaspoon ground coriander
1¼ lbs. lean lamb, cut into 1½-inch cubes
Salt and freshly ground black pepper
8 bay leaves
Peel of ½ preserved lemon (see page 10), cut up
TOMATO & OLIVE SALSA
6 oz. (1¼ cups) mixed pitted olives, chopped
1 small red onion, finely chopped
4 plum tomatoes, peeled and chopped
1 fresh red chile, cored, seeded and finely chopped
2 tablespoons olive oil

Mix the garlic, lemon juice, olive oil, chile, cumin and coriander in a large shallow dish. Add the lamb cubes, with pepper to taste. Mix well. Cover and leave to marinate in the refrigerator 2 hours. To make the salsa, put the olives, onion, tomatoes, chile, olive oil and pepper in a bowl. Mix well, cover and set aside.

Remove the lamb from the marinade and divide among 4 skewers, adding the bay leaves and lemon peel at intervals. Cook over a grill, on a ridged iron broiler pan or under a hot broiler, turning occasionally, 10 minutes until the lamb is browned and crisp outside and pink and juicy inside. Serve with the salsa, and with a rice pilaf.

Makes 4 servings.

Variation: Lean beef may be used instead of lamb.

MOROCCAN COUSCOUS

2¼ lbs. trimmed lamb shoulder, cut into pieces
2 onions, chopped
⅓ cup chick-peas, soaked overnight
1 teaspoon ground ginger
Salt and freshly ground black pepper
Pinch saffron threads
4 each small turnips and carrots, in large pieces
1 lb. (2½ cups) regular couscous (not instant)
2 tablespoons smen or butter, melted
A little rosewater
⅓ cup raisins
4 medium zucchini, halved lengthwise
1 butternut squash, peeled and cubed
2 tomatoes, quartered
2 tablespoons each chopped fresh cilantro and parsley

Place the lamb, with the onions and chick-peas in the bottom of a couscoussière or large stockpot. Stir in the ginger, saffron and 1 teaspoon pepper. Cover with water, bring to a boil and simmer, covered, 45 minutes. Add the turnips and carrots.

Place the couscous grains in a large bowl. Dissolve 1 teaspoon salt in ⅔ cup water and sprinkle over the couscous. Stir with your fingers, rubbing to separate the grains and break up any lumps. When the couscous has soaked up all the water, place in the top of a couscoussière, or in a colander lined with cheesecloth. Set the couscoussière or colander on top of the simmering stew.

If any steam escapes, wrap a strip of cloth around the top of the pan before placing the couscous on top. Steam, covered, 20 minutes, occasionally drawing a fork through the couscous grains to separate them. Turn the couscous out onto a large wooden or earthenware dish. Sprinkle with a little salted water, as before, and separate the grains with your fingers.

Lightly rub in the melted smen or butter and the rosewater and put the couscous back in the top part of the couscoussière or colander. Add the raisins, zucchini, squash, tomatoes, salt, cilantro and parsley to the simmering stew then replace the couscous over the pan. Steam a further 30 minutes, occasionally fluffing the couscous grains with a fork.

To serve, pile the couscous onto a large wooden or earthenware serving dish. With a slotted spoon, transfer the lamb and vegetables to to the center of the dish. Pour over some of the broth. Stir some harissa (see page 46) into the remaining broth and serve it separately.

Makes 6 servings.

Variation: The selection of vegetables can include beans, peas and eggplant, but traditionally seven vegetables are used.

POMEGRANATE LAMB

3 tablespoons vegetable oil
1 large onion, sliced
2 cloves garlic, finely chopped
1-inch piece ginger root, peeled and finely chopped
2¼ lbs. lean lamb such as shoulder or leg, cubed
Salt and freshly ground black pepper
Juice of 2 pomegranates, about 1¼ cups
1 teaspoon ground cumin
½ teaspoon ground cinnamon
¼ teaspoon ground nutmeg
3 cardamom pods, lightly crushed
½ cup Greek yogurt
Pomegranate seeds and chopped fresh mint, to garnish

Heat the oil in a Dutch oven. Add the onion, garlic and ginger and cook 10 minutes until soft. Remove from the pan and set aside. In the same pan, brown the lamb, in batches, and set aside. Return the onion, garlic, ginger and lamb to the pan. Season with salt and pepper. Gradually stir in the pomegranate juice, allowing each addition to be absorbed before adding more. There should be very little liquid left.

Add the cumin, cinnamon, nutmeg and cardamom to the pan and stir 1 minute. Stir in the yogurt. Cover the pan tightly and cook very gently, preferably on a heat diffuser, 30 to 40 minutes until the lamb is tender. Check from time to time that the lamb is not sticking and drying out too much. Add a little water, if necessary. Garnish with pomegranate seeds and chopped mint, and serve with rice.

Makes 4 to 6 servings.

—ROAST STUFFED LEG OF LAMB—

1 (4-lb.) boned leg of lamb, plus the bones
Salt and freshly ground black pepper
1 onion, quartered
7 tablespoons olive oil
3 rosemary sprigs
⅔ cup dry white wine
Juice of 2 lemons
STUFFING
¼ cup couscous
2 tablespoons olive oil
1 small onion, finely chopped
1 clove garlic, crushed
1 teaspoon ground cinnamon
1 teaspoon ground cumin
4 oz. (1 cup) ready-to-eat dried apricots, chopped
2 oz. (⅔ cup) pine nuts

To make the stuffing, place the couscous in a bowl and cover with boiling water; leave to stand until absorbed and fluff up with a fork. Heat the oil, add the onion and garlic and cook 10 minutes. Leave to cool. Stir into the couscous with the cinnamon, cumin, apricots, pine nuts, salt and pepper. Place 5 pieces of string in parallel lines on the work surface. Place the lamb, skin side down, across them and season with salt and pepper. Spoon the stuffing onto the meat. Roll up firmly and tie to make a neat shape. Preheat the oven to 475F (240C).

Roast the lamb bones and onion in a pan with 3 tablespoons of the oil 15 minutes. Add the rosemary and lamb. Pour in the wine and lemon juice, spoon over remaining olive oil and season. Roast 15 minutes, then reduce heat to 400F (200C) and cook 1 hour, basting occasionally. Remove the lamb and let stand 15 minutes. Add 2½ cups water to the pan, and boil until reduced. Serve with the lamb. Serve with a mixed salad.

Makes 6 to 8 servings.

—LAMB WITH CHICK-PEA MASH—

1 clove garlic, crushed
1 teaspoon ground cumin
1 teaspoon ground coriander
1 teaspoon paprika
1 teaspoon dried thyme
2 tablespoons olive oil
grated rind and juice of 1 lemon
2 racks of lamb, trimmed
CHICK-PEA MASH
2 x 240g cans chick-peas, drained
2 cloves garlic, crushed
juice of ½ lemon
salt and freshly ground black pepper

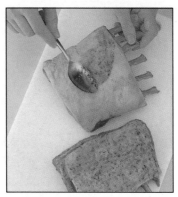

In a small bowl, mix together the garlic, cumin, coriander, paprika, thyme, olive oil, lemon rind and juice. Place the lamb in a roasting tin. Spread the spice paste over the lamb and set aside for 1 hour. Preheat the oven to 220C (425F/Gas 7). Roast the lamb in the oven for 25-30 minutes for medium rare. Allow an extra 10 minutes for medium and a further 15-20 minutes for well done. Remove the lamb from the oven, cover with foil and allow to stand for 5-10 minutes.

Meanwhile, make the chick-pea mash. Place the chick-peas, garlic, lemon juice, salt and pepper in a blender or food processor. Process until smooth, adding a little boiling water to make the desired consistency. Transfer to a saucepan and heat gently. To serve, carve the lamb into individual chops. Place a mound of chick-pea mash on each of 4 heated plates and arrange the chops on top. Serve with roasted vegetables.

Serves 4.

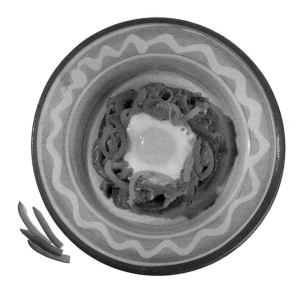

CHAKCHOUKA

2 tablespoons olive oil
1 onion, thinly sliced
1 clove garlic, crushed
1 red bell pepper, seeded and sliced
1 green bell pepper, seeded and sliced
4 merguez (Algerian) sausages, sliced
6 tomatoes, peeled and quartered
Salt and freshly ground black pepper
1 teaspoon Harissa (see page 46)
2 teaspoons chopped fresh mint
4 eggs

Heat the oil in a large skillet. Add the onion, garlic and bell peppers and cook gently 10 minutes.

Add the sausages, cook a few minutes, then stir in the tomatoes. Season with salt, pepper and harissa and cook slowly 10 more minutes until the vegetables are well blended. Stir in the mint.

Make 4 indentations in the mixture and break an egg into each one. Cover the pan and cook gently 6 to 7 minutes until the eggs are set. Divide into 4 and serve straight from the pan.

Makes 4 servings.

Variation: The eggs may be omitted and double the quantity of sausages used instead.

—BULGAR & VERMICELLI PILAF—

2 tablespoons olive oil
1 onion, thinly sliced
1 green bell pepper, seeded and sliced
1 oz. cut vermicelli
8 oz. (1¼ cups) bulgar wheat
1½ cups vegetable stock
2 tomatoes, roughly chopped
Salt and freshly ground black pepper
2 tablespoons chopped fresh flat leafed parsley
Fried onions, to garnish

Heat the olive oil in a large saucepan. Add the onion and cook 5 minutes then add the sliced bell pepper and cook until the onion is soft.

Add the vermicelli and stir to coat with oil. Put the bulgar wheat in a colander and rinse in cold water, then add to the pan. Pour in the vegetable stock and bring to a boil. Cover the pan and simmer 5 minutes.

Add the tomatoes and simmer a further 5 to 10 minutes until the bulgar wheat is tender and the stock is absorbed. Add more stock if necessary. Season with salt and pepper and stir in the parsley. Serve, garnished with fried onions.

Makes 6 servings.

——————MOROCCAN RICE——————

2 cups long grain rice
4 tablespoons butter
Pinch of saffron threads
Salt and freshly ground black pepper
½ cinnamon stick
½ cup chopped ready-to-eat dried apricots
6 tablespoons raisins
1 oz. (⅓ cup) hazelnuts
1 oz. (⅓ cup) pine nuts

Place the rice in a bowl and cover with plenty of water. Leave to soak 1 hour. Drain, rinse under cold water and drain again. Spread out on a tray to dry 30 minutes.

Melt 3 tablespoons of the butter in a large heavy saucepan. Stir in the rice and saffron. Pour 3¾ cups water over, add 1 teaspoon salt and the cinnamon stick and bring to the boil. Stir in the apricots and raisins and bring to the boil. Cover the pan then simmer on the lowest heat, without removing the lid, 15 minutes or until the rice is tender and the liquid is absorbed. Remove from the heat.

Cover the rice with a dry dish cloth and let stand 15 minutes. Melt the remaining butter in a small skillet and toss the hazelnuts and pine nuts in it until golden. Season the rice with pepper then stir in the nuts just before serving.

Makes 6 servings.

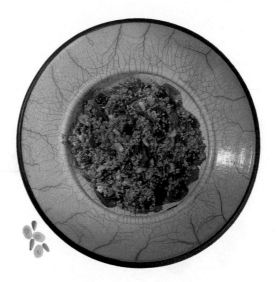

——COUSCOUS & BEET SALAD——

1 lb. (2 cups) couscous
Chicken or vegetable stock
Juice of 1 lemon
3 tablespoons olive oil, plus extra for drizzling
Salt and freshly ground black pepper
10 oz. cooked beets, cut into ½-inch cubes
4 scallions, chopped
2½ oz. baby arugula leaves
2½ oz. (¾ cup) toasted pine nuts
1 teaspoon toasted cumin seeds
1 tablespoon chopped fresh mint

Place the couscous in a bowl and pour over enough boiling stock to cover. Set aside 10 minutes until the liquid is absorbed.

Fluff up the grains of couscous with a fork. Stir in the lemon juice and olive oil and season generously with salt and pepper.

Just before serving, stir the beets into the couscous. Add the scallions, arugula leaves, pine nuts, cumin seeds and mint. Transfer to a salad bowl and drizzle a little olive oil over.

Makes 6 servings.

RICE & LENTILS

4 oz. (⅔ cup) Puy lentils
¾ cup long grain rice
2 tablespoons butter
1 red onion, finely chopped
1 clove garlic, crushed
1 teaspoon turmeric
2 teaspoons ground coriander
1 teaspoon ground cumin
1 tablespoon tomato paste
2½ cups vegetable stock
Salt and freshly ground black pepper
1 tablespoon chopped fresh cilantro

Place the lentils in a bowl, cover with boiling water and leave 30 minutes.

Rinse the rice and leave to soak 30 minutes. Heat the butter in a large saucepan. Add the onion and garlic and cook 10 minutes until soft. Stir in the turmeric, ground coriander and ground cumin and stir 1 more minute. Drain the lentils and rice thoroughly. Add to the pan and stir 1 minute.

Stir the tomato paste into the stock and pour into the rice mixture; season with plenty of salt and pepper and bring to a boil. Cover and simmer 20 minutes, or until the lentils are tender and the rice is cooked. All the liquid should have been absorbed. Stir in the fresh cilantro and serve immediately.

Makes 4 servings.

OKRA & TOMATOES

1 lb. fresh young okra
¼ cup olive oil
8 oz. white pearl onions, peeled
2 cloves garlic, crushed
1 teaspoon ground coriander
1 lb. tomatoes, peeled and chopped
1 tablespoon lemon juice
Salt and freshly ground black pepper
1 teaspoon sugar
Chopped fresh parsley, to garnish

Cut the stems off the okra. Wash the pods, drain and pat dry with paper towels. Take care not to pierce the pods.

Heat the oil in a large pan, add the onions and cook, turning frequently, 10 minutes. Add the garlic and ground coriander and cook 5 more minutes or until the onions are softened and lightly colored. Add the okra and turn carefully in the oil. Cook 5 minutes.

Add the tomatoes, lemon juice, salt, pepper and sugar. Cover the pan and simmer gently 10 minutes. Remove the lid and cook a further 10 minutes or until the okra are tender and the sauce is reduced. If the sauce reduces too quickly, add a little water. Garnish with chopped parsley and serve, hot, cold or at room temperature.

Makes 4 to 6 servings.

—POTATO & CHICK-PEA SALAD—

1 lb. small new potatoes
2 tablespoons olive oil
1 onion, sliced
2 cloves garlic, sliced
1 teaspoon cumin seeds
1 lb. plum tomatoes, peeled
1 (15-oz.) can chick-peas, drained
Salt and freshly ground black pepper
2 tablespoons roughly chopped fresh mint

Either scrub or peel the potatoes, according to preference. Cut in half unless they are very small. Boil in salted water 10 minutes or until soft. Drain.

Meanwhile, heat the oil in a large saucepan. Add the onion and cook 10 minutes until soft and golden brown. Add the garlic and cumin seeds and cook 3 or 4 minutes. Cut the tomatoes into eighths and add to the pan. Cook a few minutes until the tomatoes begin to soften.

Add the drained chick-peas and the potatoes. Cook a few minutes until warmed through. Season with salt and pepper and stir in the mint. Serve hot or cold.

Makes 4 to 6 servings.

—STUFFED VEGETABLES—

¼ cup couscous
6 sun-dried tomatoes in oil, drained and chopped
¼ cup chopped ready-to-eat dried apricots
1 tablespoon chopped fresh mint
1 tablespoon pine nuts
4 scallions, chopped
½ teaspoon ground ginger
Salt and freshly ground pepper
4 baby eggplants
4 zucchini
4 baby red bell peppers
2 tablespoons olive oil
Greek yogurt, to serve

Place the couscous in a bowl and pour ⅔ cup boiling water over.

Place the sun-dried tomatoes in a bowl with the apricots, mint, pine nuts, scallions, ginger, salt and pepper. Fluff up the couscous with a fork and add to the bowl. Mix together. Bring a saucepan of salted water to a boil. Add the eggplants, zucchini and peppers and cook 3 minutes. Drain. Preheat the oven to 400F (200C). Cut the tops off the eggplants and peppers. Cut a strip from one side of each zucchini.

Hollow out the eggplants and zucchini, leaving a shell about ¼ inch thick. Roughly chop the flesh and add to the couscous mixture. Core and seed the peppers. Stuff the vegetables with the couscous mixture. Place in a baking dish and drizzle with the olive oil. Cover the dish with foil and bake 15 minutes. Remove the foil and bake a further 10 minutes or until the vegetables are soft. Serve with yogurt.

Makes 4 servings.

—BLACK-EYED PEAS & SPINACH—

8 oz. (1¼ cups) black-eyed peas, soaked overnight
2 bay leaves
3 tablespoons vegetable oil
1 large onion, finely chopped
2 cloves garlic, crushed
1 teaspoon cumin seeds
2 teaspoons ground cumin
1 teaspoon ground coriander
4 plum tomatoes, roughly chopped
Salt and freshly ground black pepper
1 lb. fresh young spinach, washed and dried
4 tablespoons Greek yogurt
2 tablespoons chopped fresh cilantro

Drain the black-eyed peas and place in a saucepan with the bay leaves. Cover with cold water and bring to a boil. Boil rapidly 10 minutes then skim off any scum from the surface. Cover, and simmer 30 to 35 minutes until the peas are tender. Drain, reserving the cooking liquid. Heat the oil in a large pan. Add the onion and cook 10 minutes until soft and lightly colored. Add the garlic and cumin seeds and cook until the seeds begin to pop. Add the ground cumin and coriander and cook, stirring, 1 minute.

Add the tomatoes and drained peas and enough reserved cooking liquid just to cover. Season generously with salt and pepper and simmer until reduced and the tomatoes are soft. Check the seasoning, adding more salt, if necessary. Stir in the spinach and cook until the leaves wilt. Stir in the yogurt and chopped cilantro, bring to a boil and stir well. Serve immediately.

Makes 6 servings.

Variation: To save time, use canned peas.

FRIED BABY CARROTS

1 lb. baby carrots
3 tablespoons olive oil
1 clove garlic, crushed
1 teaspoon sugar
Grated rind of 1 lemon
Juice of ½ lemon
Salt and freshly ground black pepper
2 tablespoons roughly chopped fresh mint
Sprigs of mint, to garnish

Peel the carrots and trim them, leaving some green tops. If the carrots are bigger than the width of a finger, halve them lengthwise.

Heat the oil in a skillet large enough to hold the carrots in a single layer. Add the carrots and cook gently 15 minutes, shaking frequently. Add the garlic and cook a further 10 minutes until the carrots are tender and flecked with brown.

Add the sugar and cook 2 minutes to caramelize slightly. Stir in the lemon rind and juice and season with salt and pepper. Stir in the chopped mint and transfer to a serving dish. Garnish with sprigs of mint.

Makes 4 servings.

──────BROILED VEGETABLES──────

¼ cup couscous
1 red bell pepper, seeded and cut into quarters
2 baby zucchini, cut in half lengthwise
2 baby eggplants, cut in half lengthwise
1 fennel bulb, cut into quarters
4 pattypan squashes
2 tablespoons olive oil
Sprigs of mint and lemon slices, to garnish
MARINADE
⅔ cup olive oil
1 tablespoon lemon juice
2 cloves garlic, crushed
Salt and freshly ground black pepper
1 teaspoon chopped fresh parsley
1 teaspoon chopped fresh mint

Place the couscous in a bowl and cover with boiling water. Leave 10 minutes to absorb the water then fluff up with a fork and spread out in a dish. Leave 1 hour to dry. To make the marinade, in a large bowl, mix together the olive oil, lemon juice, garlic, salt, pepper, parsley and mint. Place the red bell pepper in the bowl with the marinade. Add the zucchini, eggplants, fennel bulb and squashes. Marinate 1 hour. Preheat a broiler or grill.

Broil the vegetables, turning and brushing with the marinade every few minutes, 10 minutes, or until tender and lightly browned. If using a ridged broiler pan, broil them in batches; keep them warm while the remainder are broiling. Heat the olive oil in a skillet. Add the couscous and fry, stirring, until golden and crisp. Transfer the vegetables to a heated serving dish and scatter the couscous over. Serve, garnished with mint leaves and lemon slices.

Makes 4 servings.

SWEET & SOUR ZUCCHINI

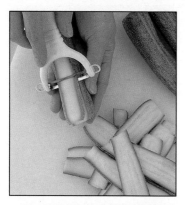

1 lb. small zucchini
3 tablespoons olive oil
2 cloves garlic, crushed
Juice of 1 lemon
2 teaspoons soft brown sugar
3 tablespoons chopped almonds
¼ cup raisins
Salt and freshly ground black pepper
Lemon slices, to garnish

Trim the zucchini and cut into long thin slices or ribbons, using a potato peeler.

Heat the oil in a large skillet. Add the garlic and cook 2 minutes. Add the zucchini and stir until coated with oil. Stir in the lemon juice, brown sugar, almonds, raisins, salt and pepper.

Simmer, stirring, 5 to 10 minutes, until the zucchini are cooked. If there is too much liquid in the pan, increase the heat 1 to 2 minutes to allow it to evaporate. Serve, garnished with lemon slices.

Makes 4 servings.

Variation: Other vegetables such as leeks and baby onions are suitable for cooking in this way.

—MOROCCAN CARROT SALAD—

1 lb. carrots
2 teaspoons honey
3 tablespoons olive oil
Juice of ½ lemon
1 tablespoon rosewater
⅓ cup raisins
½ teaspoon ground cinnamon
Salt and freshly ground black pepper
3 oz. (¾ cup) sliced almonds

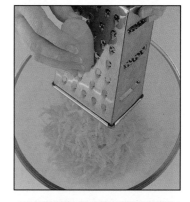

Peel and trim the carrots and grate coarsely into a bowl.

Stir in the honey, olive oil, lemon juice, rosewater, raisins and ground cinnamon. Season with salt and pepper and mix well.

Leave at room temperature 1 hour for the flavors to blend together. Stir in the sliced almonds and transfer to a serving dish

Makes 4 servings.

—LENTIL & TOMATO SALAD—

8 oz. (1¼ cups) green lentils
¼ cup olive oil
1 onion, finely chopped
2 cloves garlic, crushed
4 plum tomatoes, peeled and chopped
Salt and freshly ground black pepper
1 tablespoon chopped fresh parsley
2 tablespoons lemon juice
Strips of lemon rind and chopped scallions, to garnish

Place the lentils in a bowl, cover with cold water and leave to soak 3 to 4 hours. Drain well.

Heat half the oil in a large saucepan, add the onion and garlic and cook 10 minutes or until soft. Add the tomatoes, cook 1 minute, then add the lentils. Cover with water. Cover the pan and simmer gently 30 minutes, adding water if necessary, until the lentils are tender and all the water has been absorbed. The lentils should still hold their shape.

Add salt, pepper, parsley, lemon juice and the remaining oil. Mix carefully, then transfer to a serving dish and leave to cool. Serve, garnished with strips of lemon rind and chopped scallions.

Makes 4 to 6 servings.

—BROILED EGGPLANTS & LABNA—

2 medium eggplants, thickly sliced
3 tablespoons olive oil
8 oz. cherry tomatoes
1 recipe Labna (see page 26)
2 tablespoons toasted pine nuts
Sprigs of cilantro, to garnish
DRESSING
½ cup olive oil
Juice of 1 lemon
2 tablespoons chopped fresh cilantro
Salt and freshly ground black pepper

Brush the eggplant slices with olive oil and broil on a preheated ridged iron grill pan or under a broiler, 5 minutes or until brown.

Turn, brush with more oil and broil a few more minutes until tender and browned. Transfer to a serving dish and let cool. To make the salad dressing, place the olive oil, lemon juice, cilantro, salt and pepper in a bowl and whisk together.

Pour some of the dressing over the eggplants. Halve the tomatoes and cut the labna into slices or cubes. Arrange the tomatoes and labna over the eggplant slices. Pour the remaining dressing over. Scatter the pine nuts on top and serve, garnished with sprigs of cilantro.

Makes 4 servings.

Variation: Feta makes a good alternative to the labna.

BLACK-EYED PEA SALAD

12 oz. (2 cups) black-eyed peas, soaked overnight
Salt
1 red onion, chopped
Red bell pepper strips, to garnish
DRESSING
½ cup olive oil
Juice of 1 lemon
1 clove garlic, crushed
4 tablespoons chopped fresh flat leaf parsley
1 teaspoon ground cumin
½-1 teaspoon Harissa (see page 46)

Drain the peas and place in a large saucepan. Cover with water and bring to a boil.

Boil briskly 10 minutes then simmer, covered, 20 minutes, or until tender. Add salt towards the end of the cooking time. Drain the peas and place in a large bowl. To make the dressing, place the oil, lemon juice, garlic, parsley, cumin and harissa in a bowl and whisk together. Pour the dressing over the warm peas.

Add the chopped onion and mix well. Leave until cold, then transfer to a serving dish. Serve the salad garnished with strips of red bell pepper.

Makes 6 servings.

Variation: Beans, such as flageolet or red kidney beans may be used instead of, or combined with, black-eyed peas.

–TOMATO, OLIVE & CAPER SALAD–

6 oz. (1¼ cups) pitted mixed olives
2 anchovy fillets
6 tablespoons olive oil
1 tablespoon lemon juice
2 tablespoons capers
2 tablespoons roughly chopped fresh cilantro
1 clove garlic, crushed
1 lb. plum tomatoes
Salt and freshly ground black pepper
Grated lemon rind, to garnish

Place ¾ cup of the olives in a food processor or blender with the anchovies, 2 tablespoons of the olive oil and the lemon juice.

Process a few seconds to a coarse dressing. Transfer the mixture to a bowl, add the capers, chopped cilantro and garlic and set aside. Cut the tomatoes into rough chunks. In a skillet, heat the remaining oil. Add the tomatoes and cook briefly until just beginning to soften.

Add the olive mixture and reserved olives and heat 1 minute until warmed through. Season with pepper. Garnish with with grated lemon rind and serve with salad greens.

Makes 4 servings.

—WATERMELON & FETA SALAD—

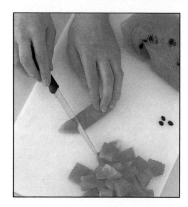

1 (1⅓-lb.) piece watermelon
4½ oz. feta cheese
Freshly ground black pepper
12 pitted black olives
2 tablespoons roughly chopped fresh mint
2 tablespoons olive oil
2 teaspoons lime juice

Cut the rind off the watermelon and cut the melon into cubes, picking out and discarding the seeds.

Arrange the melon cubes on a serving dish. Roughly crumble the feta cheese over the melon. Sprinkle with freshly ground black pepper. Arrange the olives on top.

Scatter the chopped mint over. Mix together the olive oil and lime juice and drizzle over the salad.

Makes 4 servings.

Variations: Sliced radishes or pomegranate seeds may be added to this traditional salad.

—TUNISIAN ORANGE SALAD—

6 small oranges
1 fennel bulb
1 red onion
1 tablespoon cumin seeds
1 teaspoon coarsely ground black pepper
1 tablespoon chopped fresh mint
6 tablespoons olive oil
Fresh mint sprigs and black olives, to serve

Cut the peel off the oranges, removing all
the pith. Thinly slice the oranges, catching
any juice.

Cut the fennel in half and slice it thinly.
Slice the onion thinly. Arrange the orange,
fennel and onion slices in a dish, sprinkling
each layer with cumin seeds, black pepper,
mint and olive oil. Drizzle the reserved
orange juice over.

Leave the salad to marinate in a cool place
1 to 2 hours. Just before serving, scatter the
salad with mint sprigs and black olives.

Makes 6 servings.

Note: Leaving the salad to marinate up to 2
hours allows the flavors to develop and the
onion to soften. However, do not leave the
salad longer than this before serving.

—CASABLANCA FRUIT SALAD—

4 oranges
2 peaches
4 figs
2 pomegranates
1 tablespoon orange flower water
Powdered sugar

Carefully cut the peel off the oranges, removing any pith. Cut the oranges into segments by cutting down between the membranes with a sharp knife. Reserve any juice in a bowl. Place the orange segments in a serving dish.

Place the peaches in a bowl and cover with boiling water. Leave 30 seconds, then plunge into cold water 30 seconds. Peel off the skins. Carefully cut the peaches into wedge-shaped slices down to the seed; add the peach slices to the oranges. Cut the figs lengthwise into wedges and add to the prepared fruit.

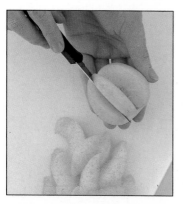

Halve the pomegranates and scoop out the seeds. Place about two-thirds of the seeds in a food processor and blend 2 to 3 seconds to extract the juice. Strain through a nylon sieve into the bowl of reserved orange juice. Stir in the orange flower water and sugar, to taste, and pour over the fruit. Scatter the remaining pomegranate seeds over and serve.

Makes 4 to 6 servings.

—STUFFED DATES & WALNUTS—

12 fresh dates
1½ oz. (½ cup) ground almonds
2 tablespoons very finely chopped pistachio nuts
2 tablespoons granulated sugar
Orange flower water
24 walnut halves
Powdered sugar, to decorate

With a sharp knife, make a slit down the length of each date and carefully remove the seed.

In a bowl, mix together the ground almonds, chopped pistachio nuts and granulated sugar. Add enough orange flower water to make a smooth paste. Shape half of the paste into 12 nuggets the size of date seeds and use to stuff the dates.

Use the remaining paste to sandwich the walnut halves together in pairs. Sift a little powdered sugar over the stuffed dates and walnuts and serve with coffee.

Makes 4 to 6 servings.

—PEACHES IN CINNAMON SYRUP—

2 oz. (⅓ cup) blanched almonds
4 oz. (¾ cup) shelled pistachio nuts
½ teaspoon ground cinnamon
2 tablespoons sugar
1 egg yolk
6 ripe but firm peaches, halved and seeded
Greek yogurt, to serve
CINNAMON SYRUP
3 tablespoons honey
2 cinnamon sticks
2 tablespoons rosewater

Coarsely chop the almonds and pistachio nuts in a food processor, then stir in the cinnamon and sugar.

Stir in the egg yolk and mix to a paste. Preheat the oven to 350F (180C). Spoon the mixture into the peach halves and arrange the fruit closely in a baking dish. To make the cinnamon syrup, place the honey in a saucepan with 1¼ cups water. Heat gently to dissolve the honey.

Add the cinnamon sticks and boil 5 to 6 minutes until slightly thickened. Add the rosewater and pour the syrup round the peaches. Bake 15 to 20 minutes until the peaches are tender but not falling apart. Baste occasionally with the syrup. Serve with yogurt.

Makes 6 servings.

—SWEET DESSERT COUSCOUS—

1 cup plus 2 tablespoons couscous
⅔ cup fresh dates
⅔ cup ready-to-eat prunes
6 tablespoons butter, melted
¼ cup sugar
1 teaspoon ground cinnamon
½ teaspoon ground nutmeg
Rose petals, to decorate

Place the couscous in a bowl and cover with ⅔ cup warm water. Leave 15 minutes to swell.

Halve each date lengthwise, remove the seed and cut into 4 pieces. Roughly chop the prunes. Fluff up the grains of couscous with a fork then place in a couscoussière or in a cheesecloth-lined colander and steam over simmering water 15 minutes until hot.

Transfer to a bowl, fluff up again with a fork. Add the melted butter, sugar, dates and prunes. Pile the couscous in a cone shape in a serving dish. Mix the cinnamon and nutmeg together and sprinkle in delicate trails over the couscous. Serve, decorated with rose petals.

Makes 4 servings.

──ORANGE & ALMOND CAKE──

1 orange
½ cup butter, softened
½ cup granulated sugar
2 eggs, beaten
1 cup semolina
3½ oz. (1 cup) ground almonds
1½ teaspoons baking powder
4 oranges, peeled and sliced
⅔ cup pitted dates, roughly chopped
Powdered sugar, to decorate
SYRUP
1¼ cups orange juice
½ cup granulated sugar

Preheat the oven to 350F (180C). Butter and base line an 8-inch cake pan.

Grate the rind from the orange, and squeeze the juice from one half. In a bowl, beat together the butter, orange rind and granulated sugar until light and creamy. Gradually beat in the eggs. Mix together the semolina, ground almonds and baking powder and fold into the creamed mixture with the reserved orange juice. Spoon the mixture into the prepared pan and bake 30 to 40 minutes until well risen and a skewer inserted into the center comes out clean. Leave to cool in the pan a few minutes.

Meanwhile, make the syrup. Put the orange juice and sugar in a pan; heat gently until the sugar dissolves. Bring to a boil and simmer 4 minutes until syrupy. Turn the cake out onto a deep serving dish. Using a skewer, make holes in the warm cake. Spoon three-quarters of the syrup over and leave 30 minutes. Place the sliced oranges and dates in the remaining syrup and let cool. Dust the cake with powdered sugar and cut into slices. Serve with the fruit in syrup.

Serves 8.

-PISTACHIO & HAZELNUT ROLLS-

2 oz. (½ cup) coarsely ground pistachio nuts
2 oz. (½ cup) ground hazelnuts
¼ cup granulated sugar
1 tablespoon orange flower water
6 sheets filo pastry, 16 x 12 inches
¾ cup unsalted butter, melted
Powdered sugar, to decorate

Preheat the oven to 350F (180C). Grease 2 baking sheets. In a bowl, mix together the ground pistachio nuts, ground hazelnuts, granulated sugar and orange flower water.

Cut each sheet of filo pastry across into four rectangles. Pile on top of each other and cover with a dish cloth to prevent them drying out. Working with one filo rectangle at a time, brush the pastry with melted butter; spread a heaped teaspoonful of filling along the short end.

Fold the long sides in, slightly over the filling. Roll up from the filled end. Place on a prepared baking sheet with the seam underneath and brush with melted butter. Repeat with the remaining pastry and filling. Bake in the oven 20 minutes or until crisp and lightly colored. Transfer to wire racks to cool. Sift powdered sugar over.

Makes 24.

—MARRAKESH SERPENT CAKE—

12 sheets filo pastry, 16 x 12 inches
¼ cup unsalted butter, melted
Powdered sugar for dusting
Ground cinnamon, to decorate
ALMOND FILLING
8 oz. (2 cups) ground almonds
¾ cup powdered sugar
Grated rind of 1 orange
2 tablespoons orange juice
½ teaspoon almond extract
¼ cup butter, softened

To make the filling, mix the almonds, sugar, orange rind and juice, almond extract and butter. Cover and chill 30 minutes.

Preheat the oven to 350F (180C). Dust a work surface with powdered sugar. Divide the almond filling into 3 pieces and roll each piece into a rope 20 inches long. Brush 2 sheets of filo pastry with melted butter and place side by side, with the long sides overlapping slightly. Place 2 more buttered sheets on top. Lay a roll of almond filling along one of the long sides and roll up. Place a hand at each end of the roll and press in gently. Brush with butter and roll into a tight coil. Place the coil on a baking sheet.

Make two more rolls in the same way. Join them to the coil, continuing the shape and sealing the ends with water. Bake 20 to 30 minutes until crisp and golden. Invert onto another baking sheet and return to the oven a further 10 minutes to brown and crisp the other side. Invert onto a serving dish and leave to cool. Thickly sift powdered sugar over the cake then sprinkle ground cinnamon from between finger and thumb in thin zigzags across the cake.

Makes 6 to 8 servings.

—ARAB PANCAKES WITH HONEY—

4 cups bread flour
1 package active dried yeast
1 teaspoon sugar
1 egg, beaten
2½ cups warm water
Vegetable oil for shallow frying
½ cup honey
2 teaspoons orange flower water
Butter, to serve

Sift the flour into a large bowl and stir in the dried yeast and caster sugar. Mix the egg with half the water and gradually stir into the flour.

Gradually stir in the remaining water, beating well until the batter is smooth and creamy. Cover the bowl with a damp dish cloth and leave in a warm place 1 hour or until the batter rises and bubbles. When the batter is ready, lightly oil a heavy skillet. Heat the skillet until it is very hot, then reduce to a medium heat. Drop 3 tablespoons of batter into the pan. It should not spread out too much. Fry until bubbles burst on the surface of the pancake and it comes away easily from the pan.

Turn it over and cook the other side until lightly browned. Place the cooked pancakes in a heatproof dish in overlapping circles and keep warm while cooking more pancakes. In a small saucepan, gently heat the honey. Stir in the orange flower water. Serve the pancakes with a pat of butter and the warm honey.

Makes 4 to 6 servings.

Variation: These pancakes are often served layered with clotted cream.

FIG TARTS

12 oz. ready-made puff pastry
Powdered sugar for dusting
9 oz. marzipan
12 fresh figs
1 tablespoons honey

Preheat the oven to 400F (200C). On a floured surface, roll out the pastry to a thickness of ¼ inch.

Cut out six 5-inch pastry circles and place on a baking sheet. Dust a work surface with powdered sugar and roll out the marzipan to a rectangle 12 x 8 inches. Cut out six 4-inch circles and place one on each pastry circle.

Slice the figs thinly across and arrange overlapping slices on the marzipan circles (2 figs to each tart). Bake in the oven 25 minutes or until the pastry is risen and golden. Brush the tops of the tarts with honey and serve, warm or cold.

Makes 6 servings.

POMEGRANATE SORBET

1 cup granulated sugar
4-6 large pomegranates
Juice of 1 pink grapefruit
1 egg white
Pomegranate seeds and mint sprigs, to decorate

Turn the freezer to its coldest setting. Put the sugar and 1¼ cups water in a saucepan. Heat gently until the sugar has dissolved then bring to a boil and simmer 5 minutes. Let cool.

Cut the pomegranates in half and squeeze on a lemon squeezer to yield 1¾ cups juice. Strain the juice into the cooled syrup. Stir in the grapefruit juice. Pour into a freezer-proof container. Place in the freezer. When the sides are beginning to set, transfer the mixture to a bowl and beat thoroughly, or process in the food processor or blender. Return to the container and freeze 30 to 40 minutes.

When the sorbet is just beginning to solidify, whisk the egg white until stiff. Beat the sorbet mixture again until smooth. Fold in the egg white. Return to the freezer until firm. Transfer the sorbet to the refrigerator 20 minutes before serving. Serve, decorated with pomegranate seeds and mint sprigs.

Makes 4 to 6 servings.

INDEX